herbes de provence

herbes de provence

ANTHONY GARDINER
PHOTOGRAPHY BY JOHN FREEMAN

Trafalgar Square Publishing

To Jan and Colin Ross-Munro
with many thanks for setting me on the trail of les herbes de Provence

First published in the United States of America in 2002 by
Trafalgar Square Publishing, North Pomfret, Vermont 05053

Printed and bound in Malaysia by Times Offset

2 4 6 8 10 9 7 5 3 1

Text and photography © 2002 Anthony Gardiner and John Freeman
Copyright © 2002 New Holland Publishers (UK) Ltd

ISBN: 1 57076 217 1

Library of Congress Catalog Card Number: 2001093705

Designed by Blackjacks

Editor: Annie Lee
Map artwork: Amzie Viladot
Editorial direction: Rosemary Wilkinson

Reproduction by COLOURSCAN

Notes:

Any plant substance, whether used in food or medicine, externally or internally, can cause an
allergic reaction in some people. Neither the author nor the publishers can be held responsible
for claims arising from the mistaken identity of any herbs, or their inappropriate use.

Unless otherwise indicated, all recipes are to serve four.

All-purpose flour is sifted, unless specified, and measured
by dipping the cup measure into the bag and leveling.

Anthony Gardiner would like to thank all his new found friends in France who have been of invaluable help in the making of this book. In particular Michèle and Didier de la Clergerie, Esther Laushway, Amelia St. George, Colette and Michel Blanchard. He would also like to thank Mary Harding and Claudine Cassel for their work in translating recipes and turning his English into acceptable French. His best friend and wife, Jane for always being there just when he needed her most. His dear cooks, Shona Bigland and Clare Johnston who recreated the recipes so that they are accessible to anyone with a kitchen. To John Freeman's assistant Tiphaine, who became his invaluable guide to the nuances of the French language and Provence way of life. Also heartfelt thanks to Annie Lee for her professional approach to the onerous task of checking his copy and arranging the recipes so beautifully with such good humor and fun. To Jonathan and Jack whose skill and imagination have helped so much in the design. Others who have made the journey through this book a pleasant one have been: Mary Omond, Sarah and David Mertens, all the staff and management at all the restaurants in this book and, of course, his dear colleague and fellow traveller, who just happens to be the best photographer he knows, John Freeman.

John Freeman warmly thanks the many people who have made this book possible. In particular Jan and Colin Ross-Munro for their hospitality in Provence and for introducing him to Michèle and Didier de la Clergerie whose help and friendship were invaluable. To his dearest friend Amelia St. George, for her warm friendship and generosity in both hospitality and knowledge of Provence. To Alex Marcar for his generosity and hospitality. To Esther Laushway for an invaluable introduction. To all the chefs for their friendship, patience and dedication. All of them were an inspiration. To Tiphaine Popesco, his assistant throughout the year in Provence, whose friendship, loyalty and dedication constantly kept his spirits high and without whom this book would have been extremely difficult to complete. Truly a talent for the future. And, of course, Anthony, whose initial idea it was and without whom the white napkin would never be the same again!

contents

introduction

Visit a market place or souvenir shop in Provence and you will certainly come across a small packet of herbs with the label "Herbes de Provence." Often the packaging is shaped like a small sack with a bold stencil on the front, the herbs listed on a label attached to the top. It is an easy way to remind yourself of a vacation, or all too brief a visit, to an area of France that is like no other in climate and topography. The purchaser of this little souvenir invariably holds it to their face to sniff the aroma which filters through the burlap sacking. The herbs inside are all aromatic, combined in a *mélange* of scents and flavors. The five main ingredients which commonly appear on the labels are: sage, thyme, rosemary, winter savory and marjoram. To this is sometimes added an interloper, sweet basil, a culinary favorite but not indigenous to the region. It is an annual herb from the Indian continent. The five main herbs are aromatic perennials which grow in the wild, to which I add two more indigenous perennial herbs; bay and fennel.

Provence lies below the 45th parallel, so the first thing that you notice as you travel south of Lyons is the change in light. The crisp, clear, southern light lifts the spirits. Within a short while you are in the *département* of Vaucluse and you first capture sight of the umbrella pines. With the rocky landscape come juniper bushes and olive trees and this is where the *sauvage* herbs begin to flourish. *Sauvage* means wild, and the fact that it is so close to the word savage is not completely accidental. The land, which has so often been compared by romantics to Eden, has a climate that can be both kind and cruel. The road that links north to south is the *Route du Soleil*, "the route of the sun," but it is also the funnel of the Rhône valley that provides the corridor for the unrelenting Mistral. When the Mistral blows at its peak, in the winter months, it numbs the senses and tests the resilience of both flora and fauna, and humans too. But when spring comes to Provence, then all that is bountiful comes with it. The sun warms the air so quickly that you can almost see the plants growing. It is the sun and the light that make it a haven for aromatic herbs.

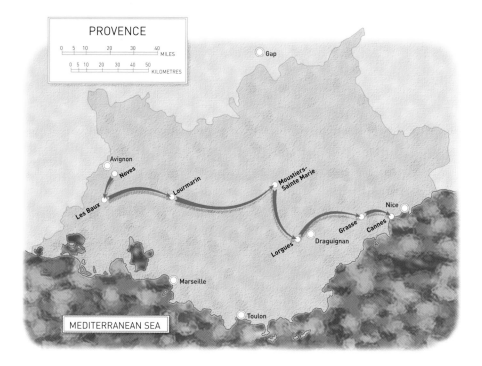

When I first created a herb garden in the Var region, I was astonished at the rate of growth of the herbs after planting. It was as if, upon placing their roots in the soil, some magic took place, and although I considered it miraculous to see prostrate rosemary bushes flowering profusely in their first year, for them it was quite natural. The black bees that came to take the pollen from the flowers appeared frighteningly large, but benign. The water, which was so necessary to survival, flowed out of the hillsides and was easily channelled into basins which were constantly replenished. The rain that came, sometimes in a mighty downpour, never lasted for long, and was quickly forgotten in a day of such brilliant sunshine that it stunned the senses. I thought I had found paradise, where every twig might grow into a tree, and seeds would sprout into maturity overnight.

But then, herbs are great survivors. For centuries they have resisted the changes in the environment that wipe out lesser plants. They go back beyond biblical times and their seeds have been found buried alongside primitive skeletons. The wonder of these plant forms is that they are, when broken down into their constituent parts, the most complex of structures. The medicinal qualities, referred to as their virtues, transform a dish into a life-enhancing experience. Anything that does us good enriches our lives and I can think of nothing more enriching than sophisticated French cuisine.

Taking seven herbs from Provence, seven restaurants of distinction, seven top chefs of immense talent, with a passion for food, and seven dishes dedicated to one particular herb at each venue, I have moved on from the garden to the dining-room and discovered the most obvious reason for cultivating these versatile herbs.

The influence of early Christian settlers was enormous in shaping the character of Provence, leaving behind villages and towns dedicated to saints and martyrs. Much of this colonization was anything but peaceful, but those that introduced a civilizing influence coupled it with the knowledge of local plants. So began a culinary tradition that is still developing. The essence of Provençal cuisine is in its use of local quality produce. Visit these restaurants and sample their dishes and you will see that the use of olive oil, the freshness of market vegetables, the natural feeding methods of livestock and the abundance of seafood so close to their shores goes towards a cuisine to be envied. Add the life-enhancing goodness of the herbs of Provence and you begin to understand why it is that this region above all others has attracted so many visitors to its restaurants.

When John Freeman and I first discussed the idea of opening up that little bag of herbs and explaining their individuality and character, little did we realize the complexity of tastes we would encounter. Each restaurant and each chef taught us the delights of being Provençal. The herbs are indigenous, but can be grown elsewhere. The produce is obtainable elsewhere, but what can't easily be experienced is the feeling you get when you are there. The warmth of the people mirrors the warmth of the land, and together with their desire to share their skill in the kitchens with us, we found a recipe for human happiness.

the herb
thyme
at auberge de noves

Thyme is one of the most versatile herbs of the Labiatae family, a family that includes marjoram, rosemary and winter savory. From the low-growing wild thyme, known as *Thymus serpyllum* has developed an upright form most common in our gardens, going under the name *Thymus vulgaris*. This common, or garden, thyme is the one used most for culinary purposes, in spite of there being over 120 cultivated forms.

According to legend, thyme came into existence on hillsides dampened by Helen of Troy's tears. Maybe this was why the Greeks burned it on their altars as an offering to the gods. Roman women used it to perfume oils and toilet water as aids to beauty, and both Romans and Greeks used it in their cooking. In Provence they went so far as to create a liqueur called "Farigoule," which has the reputation around the local market towns of St-Rémy-de-Provence and Fontvieille of being powerful enough to dissolve kidney stones.

Certainly thyme is capable of enhancing and changing the character of cooked meats. Robert Lalleman, chef at the Auberge de Noves, feels a strong link through thyme with a past age. "Whenever he eats meat, the gastronome returns to a far-distant, pre-historical past," he says seriously, "when survival was dependent on co-operation with the tribe." He believes that in the early Mediterranean-Graeco-Roman civilization which had such an influence on the development of Provençal culture, thyme played a big part in communication and the exchange of ideas. Early doctors, such as Theophrastus and Dioscorides, looked upon it as a calming herb. M. Lalleman feels it has a place in every sideboard as a herbal tea to heal a cross word or smooth over a dispute in the home. In his words,

"Le thym est l'avocat qui plaide les petites causes au cours des grands procès devant le Tribunal de la famille et du clan." "Thyme is the advocate who pleads the small cases that affect all aspects of family life."

cultivation

Both *Thymus vulgaris* and *T. serpyllum* are hardy perennials and can be grown very easily providing the soil is well drained and the aspect sunny. They both grow from seed and soft-wood cuttings. Cuttings are best taken before flowering in early spring or later in the season when they can be overwintered ready for planting the following year. *T. vulgaris* is the common upright form growing to a height of 12 to 18 inches. And *T. serpyllum* is the low-growing form, so named after its serpent-like growth on shale-covered hillsides where snakes love to bask in the warm sunshine. It is best to cut the flowers soon after they have seeded in order to promote leaf growth. Thyme loathes damp conditions, and should be kept free of encroaching leaves from other plants which might smother it in a prolonged wet spell. It is beneficial to its root growth to incorporate a little shingle or grit into the soil before planting.

culinary uses

Thyme as a tisane has the ability to revitalize the spirit and refresh the senses. The monks of the Benedictine order certainly realized this when they made it one of the prime ingredients of their famous liqueur. As M. Lalleman points out, thyme is essential to all meats, particularly mutton and pork as it aids the digestion of fats. Cut finely into omelettes, in poultry stuffings and as an addition to vegetables, thyme, providing it is used sparingly, is a welcome addition. Thyme is also an essential ingredient of a *bouquet garni*.

the restaurant
auberge de noves

Monsieur André Lalleman informed me, with a smile, that the Auberge de Noves was owned by three generations of his family. His father Robert, himself and his son, also named Robert, the present *chef de cuisine*. He looked serious for a moment and then said quietly, "My father is outside." It was late in the evening and the air had turned chilly. I looked concerned. "Don't worry," he cried cheerily, "he is buried in the grounds." Robert's father has a wicked sense of humor, and his manner of greeting makes you feel as if you have known him all your life.

The Auberge de Noves was built originally under the name Domaine de Dèves and became Auberge de Noves when Robert and Suzanne Lalleman bought it and converted it into a restaurant in 1955. They are both laid to rest in the grounds of the house with their favorite dog, Scotch, at their feet. Near them is a large dovecote, and pathways everywhere lead you between small gardens and ponds.

The wine cellar is enormous and takes up nearly all the space under the house. These cellars used to be the old kitchens and must have been terribly dark and difficult to work in. Today the kitchens are upstairs, approached through a remote-controlled sliding door, with an olive tree motif upon it, only a short walk from the dining-room. Arriving guests get a tantalizing glimpse of the chefs at work, through a glass door leading from the courtyard. By the reception desk there is an engraving of the famous poet Petrarch's life-long love, Laura de Noves. He was reputed to have first set eyes on her on Good Friday, 1327, outside the convent church of Sainte-Claire in Avignon.

All around the Auberge the countryside is dotted with beehives and vines. M. Robert Lalleman informed me that wild thyme and rosemary grow on the hill nearby. So, that morning I climbed up the steep tree-lined slope of the hill to a plateau beneath which, on the south-facing slopes, the heavy scent of wild thyme filled the air with its perfume, and a blanket of mauve-pink flowers attracted scores of honey bees. On my way back to the Auberge I found prostrate rosemary bushes crouching against the side of the shale-covered slope, where they bore the brunt of the unrelenting Mistral wind.

Back in the shade of the flat-canopied plane trees, on the terrace of this elegant house, with its cool stone water basins containing trout and langoustines waiting for their turn in the kitchens, I sat and drank a refreshing Kir royale. Last night it rained. Heavy rain that hurled itself against the walls, and now the Auberge looked as if it had been given a good wash and scrub. The sun reflected strongly off the white stone balustrades of the terrace and the soft-green, painted shutters were a welcome relief from the glare. In the dining-room the flower-printed tablecloths were bright with morning light and I could read a carved inscription above the raised open fireplace at the far end of the room: *"Qui Boit Bon Vin, Fait Bien La Besogne."* "He who drinks good wine, eats well also." There was no doubting that.

the chef
robert lalleman

Robert Lalleman was brought up at the Auberge de Noves and his first memory of working in the kitchens was at the age of eleven when he was given the task of shelling haricots and helping the pastry chef. But it was not until he reached seventeen years of age that he began his training as a chef. From Marseille he travelled to Avignon and then to Valence before going to England to work at Le Manoir aux Quat'Saisons with Raymond Blanc. By the time he had completed his National Service he was twenty-four but he felt a lack of confidence about taking over the responsibility of the kitchen at the Auberge. "My mind was not ready," he told me.

Since then he has gained confidence working with as many as twelve staff at his command and has been responsible for achieving the Michelin star rating with his own robust style of cuisine. There is a serious side to his easy-going nature that hides a poetic streak. He is passionate about the thyme growing wild on the local hillsides. He not only believes in its versatility as a herb, but is prepared to imbue it with almost mystical properties, suggesting that the plant has a close affinity with all who come into contact with it. "In the kitchen, you can use it anywhere. It is a strong herb which is even stronger after the rains."

What I enjoyed most about M. Robert was his enthusiasm for the actual process of cooking, his delight in experimenting with the infusion, the *fumé*, the *vapeur* or the grill. Of course the preparation of the food is important, but for the chef it is the method of cooking that is equally exciting. The thrill of using their ancient charcoal grill for the first time in fifteen years, for example, or the fun of setting light to a bunch of thyme, to place in a casserole dish just prior to serving. Then when he fashioned a brush out of sprigs of thyme and basted the meat, causing it to flame on the charcoal grill, I could picture him as a young boy first experiencing the excitement of the kitchen. Robert Lalleman's humor is infectious and the twinkle in the eye shows that he has a great deal yet to surprise us with in the world of haute cuisine.

"In the Latin countries, thyme is the guarantor of communication and exchange."

Mixed shellfish steamed with thyme

bouquet de coquillages
à la vapeur de thym

A couscoussier is ideal for this recipe, but failing that you can use a saucepan and a steamer with a well-fitting lid.

ingredients

8 oysters
4 scallops in their shells
a large bunch of fresh thyme
a handful of seaweed
12 large mussels
12 large clams
12 amandes-de-mer (dog-cockles)
2¼ cups water
2¼ cups white wine
3 shallots, chopped
1¼ cups light or heavy cream

method

Open the oysters and scallops, leaving their flesh attached to the concave shells. In the steamer, spread out half the thyme and seaweed and place all the shellfish on top. Set aside.

In the lower half of the couscoussier or saucepan, put the remainder of the thyme and seaweed, the water and the white wine. Cover the pan and cook over a high heat for 10 minutes, or until reduced to about 6 tablespoons of liquid. In another saucepan simmer the shallots with the cream until the mixture has the consistency of a runny sauce. This can all be done in advance.

When ready to serve, reheat the liquid in the saucepan, place the steamer of shellfish on top, cover and cook for 5 minutes. Any mussels, etc. that are not open should be discarded. Remove any juices from the shells and add to the cream sauce. Cover again and cook for 3 minutes. Serve immediately, handing the sauce separately.

Broiled Mediterranean rascasse (red scorpion fish)

chapon de méditerranée sur le gril

Legend has it that the rascasse absorbs all the aromatic herbs that grow along the cliffs where it has its feeding grounds. For this reason it is a prime ingredient of the elaborate fish dish, *bouillabaisse,* so popular in the port of Marseille. It is a red spiny fish found only in the Mediterranean; you could substitute gurnard or red mullet.

ingredients

1 rascasse, (or red snapper or striped bass) 3 pounds, or 2 smaller fish

1 bunch of dried thyme

1¼ cups olive oil

juice of 2 lemons

16 baby leeks

1 carrot, finely chopped

1 onion, finely chopped

butter

a pinch of saffron

salt and pepper

1¼ cups white wine

¾ cup plus 2 tablespoons fish stock

method

Scale and clean the fish. Put some of the thyme, half the olive oil and half the lemon juice in a bowl, add the fish, and leave to marinate in the refrigerator for at least 2 hours, turning the fish every half hour.

Peel and wash the leeks. Cook in boiling water for 5 minutes. Drain and dry on a tea towel. Heat the grill to medium. (A barbecue is ideal for this dish.) Drain the fish and cook well on all sides, crumbling thyme over and around it regularly. Cook the carrot and onion gently in a little butter, together with the saffron and salt. When the vegetables have released their liquid, add the wine, cook until no liquid remains, then add the fish stock and continue to cook on a low heat.

As soon as the carrot and onions are cooked, stir in the remaining olive oil, then season with salt, pepper and more lemon juice and pass through a strainer. Broil the leeks quickly until they begin to char and serve with the fish, accompanied by the saffron sauce.

Broiled lobster with coral sauce

homard sous le gril, sauce coraillée

Restaurants, such as Auberge de Noves, have live lobster ready to dispatch just prior to cooking. This need not be a problem for you if you have a good local fish merchant who can supply you with fresh lobster. This is essential, as lobster will keep for a very short time, even when refrigerated.

ingredients

2¼ cups water

5 tablespoons white wine

2 carrots, sliced

2 medium yellow onions, sliced

1 bouquet garni (parsley, thyme, bay leaf)

4 live lobsters, 1 to 1¼ pounds each

14 tablespoons (1¾ sticks) butter, plus extra for frying

salt and pepper

8 small bunches of thyme

7 ounces arugula

method

Put the water and wine in a large saucepan and bring to the boil. Add the carrots, onions and bouquet garni and cook for 15 minutes. Add the lobsters and cook for 4 minutes, then lift the bodies out, leaving the pincers immersed for 4 more minutes. Remove the lobsters from the pan. Put the butter in another pan, add half the liquid from the lobster pan and leave on a low heat. Cut the lobsters in half, scoop out the coral and add. Season to taste with salt and pepper.

Heat the grill. Put each half lobster on a baking tray, placing a bunch of thyme in the hollow, with the ends tucked under the lobster meat. Stir the sauce and dribble some over each lobster. Broil for 10 minutes, basting regularly with the sauce. Remove the meat from the claws and place alongside the thyme in the heads of the lobsters.

Just before serving, pour more sauce over and flash briefly under the grill. Fry the arugula in a little butter, add to the sauce and serve.

Veal chops, gently roasted with thyme flowers

côte de veau
rôtie doucement à la fleur de thym

A perfect late spring dish making the most of thyme's flowering season, which continues into early summer.

ingredients

4 tablespoons butter

4 veal chops, about 8 ounces each

1 good bunch of flowering thyme

2 bay leaves

6 carrots with their green tops, same size as the asparagus

12 asparagus spears

salt and pepper

¼ cup white wine

7 tablespoons veal stock

method

Heat a cast-iron casserole over a high flame. Add the butter, then the veal and reduce the heat at once.

Regulate the heat so that the veal will cook without burning the butter. Add the thyme and bay leaves, and turn and baste the veal frequently for about 20 minutes.

Meanwhile, trim the carrots, leaving about 3 inches of the green tops, then scrape them. Halve the asparagus spears. Bring a pan of water to the boil. Add salt and cook the vegetables for 4 minutes. Drain on a tea towel.

When the veal is cooked, remove it to a foil-covered board. Add the vegetables to the casserole and cook very gently until tender. Remove from the pan and keep warm. Add the white wine to the pan, reduce by half then add the stock. Deglaze well with a small whisk and when the consistency is correct, pass through a strainer. Serve the veal with the vegetables and hand the sauce separately.

Beef tenderloin with thyme flowers

filet de boeuf
à la ficelle et fleur de thym

A full-bodied dish requiring a full-bodied red wine to accompany it. A good Côtes du Rhône or Gigondas would be ideal.

ingredients

1 beef tenderloin, about 1½ pounds
10 thin slices of smoked bacon
1 bunch of flowering thyme
salt and pepper
2 pounds fresh petits peas, shelled
lemon juice
olive oil
1 quart beef and vegetable stock
⅔ cup light cream
curry powder
cayenne
quatre-épices
ground cumin

method

Cut the beef tenderloin in half lengthwise to obtain 2 equal-sized pieces. Spread out the bacon slices flat, side by side, and sprinkle with the thyme flowers and pepper. Roll each piece of tenderloin in bacon and tie up with string as for a roast joint. Leave to rest in the refrigerator for a few hours.

Cook the petits peas in boiling, salted water until tender, then refresh them in cold water and drain well. Reserve a few for decoration, then purée the rest in a food processor till very smooth. Season with salt, pepper, lemon juice and olive oil. Reheat only at the last moment before serving so as to keep the bright color.

Choose a heavy-based saucepan which will hold the stock and the beef. Heat the stock to 160°F and cook the meat for 40 minutes, without allowing the temperature to rise above 160°F.

A few minutes before serving, mix the cream with the same volume of cooking liquid and simmer very gently to reduce to the consistency of a sauce. Season to taste with the piquant spices. Remove the bacon slices and serve the beef accompanied by the pea purée and the sauce.

Casseroled leg of lamb with burned thyme

gigot d'agneau en cocotte au thym brûlé

A great favorite in Provence. The insertion of the garlic under the tender skin and the flaming of the thyme make this a dish to remember.

serves
four to six

ingredients

6 cloves of garlic

1 leg of lamb, about 3 pounds

12 new potatoes

12 small artichokes

2 tablespoons olive oil

butter

salt and pepper

1 large bunch of thyme

¼ cup white wine

7 tablespoons water

¾ cup plus 2 tablespoons light cream

method

Peel the cloves of garlic and quarter each one. Make incisions all over the skin of the lamb and slide in the pieces of garlic.

Preheat the oven to 425°F. Peel the potatoes and artichokes and cut the artichokes in half.

Place the meat in an open casserole with the olive oil and a good lump of butter. Season with salt and pepper. Place in the preheated oven and cook the lamb for 40 minutes, turning the meat every 10 minutes or so and basting well each time. After the lamb has cooked for 20 minutes, add the vegetables to the casserole. Season and add a sprinkling of thyme leaves. After 40 minutes, remove the lamb to a board and cover with kitchen foil.

Return the casserole to the oven to finish cooking the vegetables. When ready, remove them to the board with the lamb. Skim the fat from the casserole, add the wine and cook until it has evaporated. Add the water and reduce again to a thin sauce consistency. Meanwhile boil the cream to reduce by half and infuse with a sprig of thyme. Season.

Return the meat and vegetables to the casserole and stir in the cream. Put the rest of the bunch of thyme on top and reheat. Just before serving, flame the thyme. Cover immediately and leave for 4 minutes. Serve in the casserole, removing the lid at the table. The burning thyme will have impregnated everything with its smoke, just what is needed to heighten the dish.

Pears and strawberries roasted with thyme honey

poires et fraises rôties au miel de thym

M. Lalleman produces his own thyme honey, which has all the warmth of the sun in it. If you wish to make your own thyme-scented honey, just warm a jar of honey naturally in the sun, add a few sprigs of flowering thyme, seal the lid tightly, and leave for two weeks, turning the jar each day, before using. Store in a cool place.

ingredients

2¼ cups water
1¼ cups sugar
4 ripe pears
2 tablespoons butter
3 tablespoons thyme honey
40 strawberries
juice of ½ lemon
lemon sorbet to serve
thin slivers of pear and sprigs of thyme to decorate

method

Put the water and sugar in a saucepan and heat until the sugar has dissolved.

Peel the pears and cook in the sugar syrup for 25 minutes. Drain well.

Heat a frying pan, melt the butter and gently turn the pears until colored. Add the honey and bring to a brisk boil. Add the strawberries and a little lemon juice.

Serve immediately after the strawberries come to the boil, accompanied by a spoonful of lemon sorbet. Garnish with thin slivers of pear and a sprig of thyme.

rosemary

at oustau de baumanière

One of the most delightful and enduring legends attached to rosemary concerns Elizabeth, Queen of Hungary, who reigned during the thirteenth century. At the age of seventy-two, crippled with rheumatism and afflicted with gout, she was reputedly given a recipe by a mysterious hermit, containing rosemary as its prime ingredient. This alcoholic elixir proved such a success that within a very short while she regained her health and mobility and appeared so beautiful that the King of Poland asked her for her hand in marriage. She refused only because she believed the hermit to have been an angel in disguise. Various recipes for "Hungary Water" have come to light since then. All contain alcohol and macerated branches of rosemary, and all claim to promote beauty and long life.

Rosemary has always had a connection with Provence. As early as 1584 in Thomas Coghan's herbal, *The Haven of Health*, it was reported, "The use of rosemary in the kitchen is well known to all men. I would the herb was as plentiful among us in England as it is in that part of France which is named Provence, where it groweth of it self without setting; and is used for common fuel." I have certainly found it to be a must for getting any fire going, the natural oils causing it to burn fiercely and quickly. Throughout France it was used as incense in the churches, gaining the name *insensier* for a time. Today you will hear it referred to as *romarin*, perhaps stemming from its Roman origins as a friendship herb. Rosemary flowers are supposed to resemble the color of the sky, cloudless and enriched by the sun, and early Christians told the tale of the Virgin Mary

placing her cloak over a rosemary bush during her
flight into Egypt, whereupon the flowers changed from
white to blue, mirroring the glory of the heavens.

Rosemary is also connected with sweet memories,
and in Stratford-upon-Avon each year on Shakespeare's
birthday branches of rosemary are carried in the
streets to keep "his memory green."

cultivation

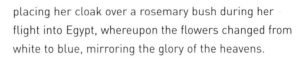

Rosemary is an evergreen shrub growing up to 6 feet in
height and can be clipped into manageable shape early
in the growing season. The erect branching stems are
covered all the way up in ovate green leaves, rich in
oils, which can be released by rubbing. It can be grown
from seed, although it is best propagated from cuttings
or from layering. Although it appears slow to grow in
the first year, once established in a well-drained, stony
soil with plenty of sun, it will become a good-sized
plant in two to three years. There are beautiful
prostrate forms in France, in particular the varieties
"Boule" and "Faranole."

culinary uses

As a digestif or as a restorative rosemary makes
a wonderful tisane. M. Charial, chef at the Oustau
de Baumanière, is well aware that it is a very strong
herb, requiring prudence in its use in the kitchen.
But it is also a surprising herb that can be used in a
marinade for strong-flavored fish such as salmon,
or with game meats such as quail or venison.
Scrambled eggs, thick soups and stews can all
benefit from the powerfully aromatic flavor of
chopped or pounded rosemary.

the restaurant
oustau de baumanière

Oustau de Baumanière owes a lot to the motor car. Without it, guests would not be able to reach it. But then that applies to so many places today. However, in 1945 when, Jean-André Charial's grandfather, Raymond Thuilier, bought this ancient farmhouse beneath the village of Les Baux, the dream he was to realize meant taking a quantum leap of courage. But this area of Provence has never been short of courageous acts. With its body firmly placed against a backdrop of grotesquely sculptured limestone forms, Oustau de Baumanière faces south down the famous Val d'Enfer, so called because of its association with Dante's *Inferno*. This is a building between a rock and a hard place, but with a soul that is soft and welcoming. The word *oustau* means a hostelry, a place to rest while the hostler tends to your horses.

After the horrors and deprivations of the Second World War people needed to begin anew, and, despite M. Thuilier's advancing years, he chose to make this place a center for Provençal hospitality to rival the best in the world. The vision was both simple and complex: to create a hotel that provided for all one's needs, comfort, quietude, leisure and above all a sophisticated cuisine that used the best-quality produce that Provence could supply. Today we have come to accept this philosophy as the norm. But it is chiefly thanks to M. Thuilier's stamina that the Relais & Châteaux chain of hotels has set a pattern for every hotel in the world.

At the heart of the Oustau are the dining-room and the kitchens. In what must have been the cellarage of the old farmhouse, there is a vaulted stone ceiling that mirrors beautifully the Renaissance palaces and Romanesque church ceilings in the adjoining village of Les Baux. Subtle up-lighting highlights the walls and makes for more intimacy. You are seated at large round tables with olive green and cream linen tablecloths, which reach to the floor. High-backed, comfortable dining-chairs support your shoulders and the simplicity of cutlery and place settings do not distract you from the most important thing: the food.

The kitchen, unusually, has only one door leading in and out, and understandably the atmosphere in there is concentrated and free of human chatter. A sign as you enter reads, *"Silence au Passe."* The only voice is that of the order chef rising above the furious sound of cooking.

Returning to the dining-room is like visiting a monastic wine-cellar where the monks have succumbed to secular delight. The outside world, seen through arched floor-to-ceiling windows, is blustery, giving warning of autumnal shocks in store. There is a sense of security accentuated by the rocks around us. M. Charial appears from the kitchen, in his chef's apparel. You feel the same sort of protection as he moves among the tables to greet you, ensuring you are feeling suitably secure with the cuisine. What his grandfather began continues, with the same *esprit*; that of the refined hostelry, where the emphasis is on the well-being of the guest.

the chef
jean-andré charial

In 1967 M. Charial, at the age of twenty-five, graduated from Paris with an H.E.C., the highest award in Business Studies. Not, you might think, the best qualification for being a chef. Yet the pull of the Oustau, and the inspiration of his grandfather, M. Thuilier, started him on course to be a master chef. Unlike some of his compatriots, he felt little desire to leave school at the age of fourteen and embark on a single career in cooking. For him there was a need to expand in other directions before realizing his vocation, and it seems to have been a wise move to make. The creative side of his nature took precedence but the business training gave him the ability to plan his ventures with an eye to profitability too. He tells me he has various sergeants in his "brigade" who allow him the space to be creative. They can, at any time, take over the running of the kitchen leaving him free to manage the other responsibilities of the hotel, including his vineyard at Romanin.

In the past five years in particular he has had the task of modernizing the cuisine of the Oustau. "Times have changed so swiftly," he tells me, "tastes have changed, with more emphasis on healthy food. More use of olive oil, less cream and most importantly taking care of your produce." This has meant going right back to the basic requirement of the earth to be fed with organic nutrition, getting right away from harsh chemicals. His passion for his cultural background is intense. "A few years ago, I set up a restaurant in London. I felt the need to escape and do my own thing. But without the local produce I could not do justice to Provençal cuisine. I was, in effect, denying my culture." He returned to the Oustau with a firm resolve to create only that which was truly Provençal, and of this particular region.

He considers his job to be seven days a week, there is no let-up, and he is constantly thinking dishes through with his team of chefs. He is rigorous in his control of the kitchen. Organization is geared to the last-minute preparation of a dish before it leaves for the table. Nothing must be missing from the plate, and with this in mind all his trainees are encouraged to plan their time efficiently. "It is no good just looking at a dish cooking for ten minutes. That time can be used to do something else in the process. Every evening is different. There is high tension to be controlled. But that is what makes it exciting. That is what energizes you."

"You must strive for simplicity, be careful not to destroy tastes, use only the best produce and grow your own vegetables."

Coconut soup with cumin, rosemary oil and Parmesan lace

soupe de cocos au cumin
à l'huile de romarin et sa dentelle au parmesan

Choose the rosemary tips with care, so as to use only the best, when making the rosemary oil.
This will ensure the purity of the color, seen through the glass.

serves
six

ingredients

8 ounces fresh coconut, chopped
1 quart chicken stock
1 pinch of cumin
2¼ cups light cream
juice of 1 lemon
7 cups loosely packed rosemary leaves
salt and pepper
2 cups grated Parmesan cheese
2¼ cups olive oil

method

Simmer the coconut in the chicken stock for 40 minutes. Add the cumin, cream, lemon juice
and 1 tablespoon of the rosemary, and simmer for a further 20 minutes to reduce. Liquefy in
a blender, then pass through a strainer. Season with salt and pepper.

Preheat the oven to 350°F. Put 6 metal rings 5 inches in diameter on baking trays. Sprinkle the
grated Parmesan inside each one. Cook in the preheated oven for 10 minutes, then remove from
the oven and leave to cool, spraying with cold water.

Warm the oil with the rest of the rosemary leaves, reserving a few for the garnish. Liquefy in a
blender and then pass through a strainer.

Serve the soup in a cup or glass. Pour over the rosemary oil and place the Parmesan lace on top,
garnished with the reserved rosemary.

Fricassée of chestnuts and Jerusalem artichokes

fricassée de châtaignes et topinambours au romarin

The sweet chestnut has always been dear to French hearts. If you are unable to find fresh chestnuts, they are available in cans. This dish follows an old tradition of mixing chestnuts, which grow on trees, with earthbound vegetables from below.

serves
six

ingredients

8 ounces chestnuts
2 pounds Jerusalem artichokes
olive oil
1 small bunch of rosemary
2¼ cups peanut oil
1 tablespoon olive oil

for the vegetable stock

1 carrot	1 leek
1 bell pepper	1 garlic clove
1 tomato	a sprinkle of thyme
1 celery stalk	1 bay leaf

method

To make the vegetable stock, put all the ingredients into a pan with 1 quart of cold water and cook very gently for 1 hour. Pass through a strainer, discarding the vegetables.

Return the stock to the pan, add the chestnuts, and cook for 10 minutes. Remove the chestnuts with a slotted spoon and keep warm. Peel all but 3 of the Jerusalem artichokes and cut them into large olive shapes. Sauté them in olive oil until lightly browned. Finish cooking them in the same vegetable stock that was used for the chestnuts. Remove with a slotted spoon and keep warm. Add a little rosemary to the stock, then simmer it until reduced by half.

Cut the reserved artichokes into very thin slices and fry them in peanut oil—not too hot— to make Jerusalem artichoke crisps.

Whisk the olive oil into the stock, then return the vegetables to the pan. Reheat and serve.

Fricassée of sole with rosemary sauce

fricassée de sole au beurre de romarin

You can, if you wish, substitute John Dory (or tilapia) for the sole, but it will not be as delicate a flavor.

serves
two

ingredients
2 soles, 10 ounces each

1 ounce carrots

2 ounces zucchini

salt and pepper

yellow bell pepper and broccoli flowerets to garnish (optional)

for the rosemary sauce

2 tablespoons finely chopped yellow onions

½ leek

1 cup button mushrooms

6 tablespoons butter

1 bouquet garni (parsley, bay leaf, celery and thyme)

1 cup white wine

2 sprigs of rosemary

method
Fillet the soles (keep the bones) and cut into narrow strips (goujonettes).

To make the rosemary sauce, chop the onions, leek and mushrooms. Sweat the fish bones gently in 2 tablespoons of butter. Add the onions, leek, mushrooms and bouquet garni and cook for a minute or two longer. Add the white wine and enough water to come halfway up the pan. Cook for 20 minutes more, then pass through a strainer. Add the rosemary sprigs to the sauce and leave to infuse for 15 minutes. Beat in the remaining butter and strain.

Slice the carrots and the zucchini and cook in boiling, salted water until tender. Poach the goujonettes of sole in the rosemary sauce and season with salt and pepper. Serve the sole in deep plates. Add the carrots and the zucchini and pour the rosemary sauce over the top. Garnish with strips of yellow bell pepper and small flowerets of steamed broccoli.

Veal sweetbreads on rosemary branches with acidulated carrot juice

ris de veau en broche de romarin
jus de carottes acidulé

Veal sweetbreads are still considered to be a great delicacy and provided they are very fresh and the membrane removed very carefully, there is no reason why they cannot provide you with a meal that just seems to dissolve in your mouth.

ingredients

4 veal sweetbreads, 7 ounces each

salt and pepper

3 tablespoons olive oil

6 tablespoons butter

1 tablespoon acacia honey

2 shallots, finely chopped

1¼ cups apple cider vinegar

1¼ cups carrot juice

1 tablespoon rosemary leaves

4 rosemary branches, each 8 inches long, blanched (optional)

method

Blanch the sweetbreads for 2 minutes in boiling, salted water. Plunge them into iced water and dry them on kitchen towels. Remove the membrane and season the sweetbreads with salt and pepper.

In a sauté pan, heat the oil and add the sweetbreads and 2 tablespoons of butter. Cook for 10 minutes, until the sweetbreads are brown on all sides. Keep them warm on a trivet over hot water, covered with a soup plate.

Pour away the oil and add another 2 tablespoons of butter to the pan with the honey and the shallots. Pour in the vinegar, then add the carrot juice and the rosemary leaves. Simmer for 5 minutes, or until reduced by half, then add the remaining butter. Pass the sauce through a strainer and keep warm.

Place a sweetbread on each serving plate and either slice, or skewer the whole sweetbread with a rosemary branch. Pour some sauce over each sweetbread and serve with, for example, some stewed bell peppers.

Turbot in rosemary marinade with roasted ceps

turbot en macération de romarin cèpes rôtis

By the time you have filleted the turbot and removed the skin you will find a great deal of weight is lost due to its heavy bones. The mushrooms can be bought in dried form.

ingredients

4 pounds turbot
2 teaspoons fresh rosemary leaves
½ cup olive oil
5 tablespoons white wine
2 tablespoons white-wine vinegar
2 shallots, finely chopped
10 peppercorns, crushed
5 tablespoons meat juices or strong meat stock
6 tablespoons butter
1½ pounds ceps (or other mushrooms), cleaned and cut into 1-inch slices
salt

method

Fillet the turbot, remove the skin and cut the fish into 4 pieces. Insert 40 of the rosemary leaves into the fish and put in a dish with 7 tablespoons of the olive oil. Cover with plastic wrap and leave to marinate for at least 3 hours and preferably overnight.

Bring to the boil the white wine, vinegar, shallots, peppercorns and remaining rosemary leaves and simmer until reduced by half. Add the meat juices or stock, then beat in 4 tablespoons of the butter. Season the sauce, then pass through a strainer and keep warm.

Fry the turbot fillets in 2 tablespoons of the marinade oil and the remaining butter for 3 minutes each side. Fry the mushrooms in the rest of the olive oil and season to taste.

Put the turbot on serving plates with the mushrooms on top and pour the sauce around.

Chicken supremes with anchovy and rosemary

suprême de volaille
à l'anchois et au romarin

Supremes, or boneless chicken breast halves, can be bought individually, but cutting them from the whole bird insures the meat remains moist and tender.

serves
two

ingredients

1 Bresse (or free range) chicken, 3½ pounds

1 carrot

1 onion

4 anchovy fillets

2 tablespoons butter

2 tablespoons chicken stock

7 ounces crème fraîche

1 cup rosemary leaves

salt and pepper

cooked asparagus, mushrooms and fava beans to garnish

2 sprigs of rosemary

method

Start by cutting the wing tips off the chicken. Remove the skin. Make a deep incision along the breastbone. Push the knife tip into the wing joint and remove the meat in one piece. This is the supreme.

Peel the carrot and onion and slice finely. Make incisions in the chicken supremes and insert small pieces of anchovy – make 5 or 6 well-spaced incisions.

Heat the butter in a saucepan and brown the supremes over a low heat. Add the carrot and onion, the chicken stock and the crème fraîche and leave to cook over a moderate heat for approximately 30 minutes until the chicken is tender. Remove the supremes from the pan and keep warm. Add the rosemary to the sauce and simmer until reduced. Strain and add salt and pepper to taste.

Cut the supremes into 4 or 5 equal pieces, place on a serving plate and pour the sauce over the top. Garnish with asparagus, mushrooms and a few skinned fava beans, and finish with a sprig of rosemary.

Brochette of fresh fruit with rosemary and vanilla

brochette de fruits frais au romarin et vanille

The addition of a grape to the otherwise square fruit is a culinary caprice. You can follow the chef's example, or substitute a round fruit of your own. A *coulis* is, quite simply, a sauce or purée.

serves
six

ingredients
7 vanilla beans
6 wooden skewers
apples, peaches, strawberries, pears, bananas and pineapples
6 grapes
6 sprigs of rosemary
rosemary honey
fruit coulis, to serve

method
Put a vanilla bean tip on the end of each skewer. Fill the skewer with alternate pieces of each fruit and finish with a grape and a sprig of rosemary.

Gently heat some rosemary honey. Open the remaining vanilla bean, scrape out the seeds and mix into the honey. Brush the fruit with this mixture and cover with plastic wrap. Leave in the refrigerator for 24 hours. Serve cold, with a fruit coulis of your choice.

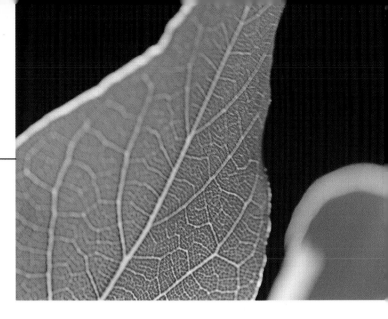

the herb
bay
at auberge la fenière

In France the school-leaving certificate is known as the *baccalauréat*, from the words *bacca laurea*, or "crown of laurel." Handed down from the Romans, this symbol of victory and reward is still used today as an accolade for poets and heroes alike. Poems in England written to celebrate royal occasions are penned by the Poet Laureate. French chefs refer to the herb as "*laurier*" so as not to confuse it with the poisonous *Prunus laurocerasus*, or Cherry laurel bush. Dedicated in ancient Rome to the sun god Apollo, bay laurel, or *Laurus nobilis*, was considered to offer protection against thunderbolts. Tiberius Caesar, supposedly, was prone to wear a crown of laurel whenever there was a thunderstorm. Pliny, from whom this fact came in his *Naturall Historie* of 77AD, also tells us, "The Laurel betokens peace insomuch as if a branch thereof be held out among armed enemies, it is a sign of quietness and a cessation from arms."

Mme Sammut at the Auberge looks upon it as a gift. A gift for the kitchen, as no *bouquet garni* is complete without it. This mixture of herbs tied in a cheesecloth bag and dipped into soups and stews is traditional in French cuisine everywhere. She particularly likes to make a skewer out of bay for adding flavor to a brochette. She also tells me that one of the best things about bay is that it doesn't wilt.

In history, the withering of bay trees has often been considered a sign of impending disaster. Just prior to the death of the emperor Nero, all the bay trees were reported to have withered to their roots, although the winter was remarkably mild. Shakespeare used this superstition in his play *Richard II*, when a Welsh army captain says, "'Tis thought the king is dead; we will not stay, The bay-trees in our country are all withered."

Because it was used by the priestesses of the Oracle at Delphi, bay has gained a reputation for conferring the gift of prophecy. Placed under a pillow, it is supposed to induce pleasant dreams.

cultivation

Bay is an evergreen with glossy aromatic leaves, small flowers and black berries which look like tiny olives. Bay trees can grow to a height of 40 feet, although in kitchen gardens they are often kept to a more manageable height, trimmed into pillar or ball shapes. They prefer full sun and a sheltered position near to the house. It is not a herb for cold climates, being a native of the Mediterranean and, as a result, should not be pruned or cut until early summer; small plants should be brought indoors before the first frosts. The best form of propagation is by taking cuttings and placing the slips in a mixture of compost and sharp sand, then leaving them in a shady place to root. The average growth rate of a bay is 1 foot a year.

culinary uses

When crushed or chopped, the leaves of bay release their rich oil, which has a strong aroma and flavor, so it is advisable to use them sparingly. Dried leaves, because they stimulate the appetite, are often added to vinegars and can be preserved in olive oil. Fresh, or dried, leaves can be added to all roasts, rice dishes, aspics and sauces. Another traditional ingredient of *bouquet garni,* bay leaves should be stored in airtight glass containers to retain their potency. The leaf should never be eaten whole, but well macerated. The whole leaf is always removed after cooking, or used for decoration.

the restaurant
auberge la fenière

Auberge La Fenière literally translated means "The hostelry where they store the hay." Animals would be housed on the floor below the hay and the farmer and his family on the floor above. The old house still has the slit windows of the storage floor which can be seen in the yard at the back. An open-sided barn is the summer kitchen, with room to seat a good-sized wedding party under one roof. The ceiling and heavy wooden beams are festooned with dried branches of wild fennel and roses. A great sheaf of lavender hangs on the wall alongside tresses of garlic. The wooden ceiling boards have been painted with whitewash, giving a feeling of space and light. The farmyard is now a quiet courtyard with tidy, low-roofed outbuildings, one of which houses a bedroom with en suite bathroom all designed to cater to the needs, if necessary, of a disabled guest. It is this sort of care and attention that Mme Sammut and her husband have gone to in setting up their restaurant on the site of the old stable block. In style, the Auberge complements the old house with its low-pitched, tiled roof, typical of the region. Just below roof level modern loggias attached to the bedrooms offer uninterrupted views of the Durance valley.

Standing on the terrace with rust-colored, triangular cut awnings fluttering above your head, it is easy to imagine yourself aboard an Arabian fishing boat. The illusion is further enhanced by the sight of decked oases on the lawns close to the restaurant. The spacious, deeply cushioned cane chairs and sofas, under pavilion shaped awnings, held aloft by angled steel struts, offer intimate islands of comfort far enough apart to make each one a private entity for animated conviviality. Here guests can meet before the meal and enjoy their aperitif, later returning for after-dinner coffee and liqueurs. Yesterday the warm wind shook the tented roofs. Today, all is peace and quiet, under a scorching sun.

Mme Sammut has collected a basket of herbs and flowers from the potager garden and a single sprig of fresh cilantro gives off its spicy perfume when she lifts it to show me. She makes for the main kitchen and I retreat to the cooler, open summer kitchen in the barn, where the chef and I quietly respect each other's space. The simmering saucepan on the stove is our only background noise. That and the soft cut of his knife peeling outsize potatoes at a massive, waist-high, chopping bench of ancient dark wood, beaten into bowed submission by years of use. The fireplace has a basket rotisserie capable of cooking fifteen gigots of lamb at once. Above it are row upon row of dark green and ocher luster jugs. This is where the staff eat, in rustic splendor, before returning to the high-vaulted, modern restaurant across the courtyard.

Cream, mushroom and soft olive greens are the colors that predominate, and soft white muslin drapes flutter along the wall of windows alongside the terrace. This indoor dining-room is theatrical and feminine, reflecting the personalities of its owners. In just four years they have created a haven where you can enjoy the best that the Lubéron has to offer. Auberge La Fenière is set to be a culinary landmark for many years to come.

the chef
reine sammut

Mme Sammut's story is a romantic one. In this land of courtly love and troubadours it seems only right that love should have determined the course of our one female chef. For if it were not so, Mme Sammut would have continued her medical studies and never discovered her true vocation. When she was a young medical student she met the aspiring musician, Guy Sammut.

"I am still in love with him," she tells me, "and through the guidance of his mother I discovered another love, the love of cooking." So began her training; working in a family kitchen, with all the intimacy that this offered. Such was her passion for the cuisine of Provence, coupled with her skill at presentation, that she went on to open a restaurant in the town of Lourmarin, gaining Michelin-starred status. She soon required more space to work in, together with a wish to have a garden to cultivate her own vegetables and herbs. This brought her to the Auberge la Fenière, where she runs her kitchen, as she describes it, "like a mother, with her children." Her own children are in their late teens and she agrees that this now gives her time to concentrate on being a top chef. "The only reason there are so few top female chefs is that it requires all your time and effort. It is a very demanding passion, and bringing up your children comes first. If I had started my restaurant when the children were so much younger I would have become frustrated by them. Now I am free to enjoy them, my husband and my cooking."

Her philosophy for the cuisine is a simple one, involving care, capability, a feminine touch, and the integration of different cultures: "This is what the Mediterranean is all about." She is always open to new ideas and encourages her brigade to be adventurous in their approach as well.

As she began cooking in a kitchen with only four women, working together, they all knew how each part of the meal was prepared. She has carried this culture on at the Auberge, and once her trainees have mastered one particular area of expertise she moves them on to another discipline. "It is vital to know as much as possible in the kitchen." To this end she requires her staff to sign on for a minimum of two years. This ensures that their "mother" gets to know them and integrates them into the family.

"I communicate through my cooking."

Goat's cheese with olive oil and herbs

fromage de chèvre
à l'huile d'olive et aux herbes

This is a traditional way of both preserving and flavoring goat's cheese. Choose a goat's cheese that is fairly dry, and a well-flavored, first cold pressing of olive oil.

Mme Reine Sammut has a *menu de dégustations* at the Auberge la Fenière, which she calls "Olive Oils and the Mediterranean," featuring among others a *fromage de chèvre à l'huile d'olive du Péloponnèse*. So there are many choices to make when looking for the right oil to complement the cheese. Like good wines, oils need to be sampled and tasted to suit your palate. But as a general guideline, if you find a well-rounded, sweet tasting oil, it should go well with these little cheeses. The highly prized accolade A.O.C., *Appelation d'Origine Contrôlée*, is awarded to growers in recognition of their good agricultural practice and guarantees you a true first pressing.

method

Put the goat's cheese in a large jar, then add a few bay leaves, one branch of thyme, one branch of savory and a few peppercorns. Cover everything with olive oil and seal the jar tightly. Leave to marinate in a cool dark place for about a week before using.

Mixed salad with bay leaf vinaigrette

mesclun de fleurs vinaigrette au laurier

Mesclun is a mixture of salad leaves consisting of arugula, purslane, watercress, corn salad, endive and dandelion. You can also add flowers of borage, marigold, begonia and pansy.

ingredients

4 handfuls of mixed salad (mesclun)

for the vinaigrette
2 tablespoons balsamic vinegar
2 bay leaves
salt and pepper
2 tablespoons good-quality olive oil

method

To make the vinaigrette, put the balsamic vinegar in a saucepan with the bay leaves. Bring to the boil, continue boiling until reduced by half, then leave to cool. Once it has cooled, add salt and pepper followed by the olive oil. Mix the salad and vinaigrette together just before serving.

Brochettes of langoustines and mackerel with bay leaves, onion compote and shellfish sauce

brochette de langoustines et maquereau au laurier
compote d'oignons et jus de crustacés

Do not be put off by this unusual combination of fish. The tastes and textures really do work, and complement each other perfectly. The bay skewers add to its completeness.

ingredients

4 bay branches, 6 inches long

2 mackerel, 13 ounces each

12 very fresh langoustines (or prawns)

2 tablespoons olive oil

for the onion compote

2 tablespoons olive oil

4 large onions, finely chopped

salt and white pepper

1 tablespoon granulated sugar

1 bay leaf

for the shellfish sauce

3 tablespoons olive oil

1 yellow onion, chopped

1 tablespoon flour

2 ripe tomatoes, chopped

1 cup white wine

2 cups water

1 bay leaf

method

To make the onion compote, heat the olive oil in a saucepan, add the onions and cook gently until soft. Season with salt and pepper, sprinkle with the sugar, and add the bay leaf. Cover the pan and cook over a low heat for 20 minutes.

Remove the bay leaves from the branches (keep the leaves for drying and storing), leaving the small topknot intact. Fillet the mackerel and cut each fillet into 3 pieces. Shell the langoustines, and de-vein them, reserving the shells for the sauce. Alternate 3 langoustines and 3 pieces of mackerel on each bay stalk. Pour 2 tablespoons of olive oil over them and refrigerate.

To make the shellfish sauce, heat the olive oil in a saucepan, add the onion and cook over a high heat until just turning brown. Add the reserved langoustine shells and, when well colored, sprinkle in the flour. Add the tomatoes, wine, water and bay leaf and season to taste. Cook for 30 minutes, then pass through a strainer into another saucepan. Return to the heat and simmer to reduce until there are about 8 tablespoons of sauce left.

Heat a non-stick frying pan and cook the brochettes on a high heat, turning them often until they are well browned on all sides. This should take no more than 6 to 8 minutes. Spoon some of the onion compote onto each plate, place a brochette on top and pour over the shellfish sauce.

John Dory with bay and a bohémienne of fennel

saint-pierre au laurier bohémienne de fenouil

In France, John Dory is known as St. Pierre because of the "thumb-marks of St. Peter" on its back. It has an excellent flavor similar to turbot. If you can't find any, substitute porgy.

ingredients

2 fennel bulbs
1 onion
1 zucchini
6 tablespoons olive oil
½ tablespoon minced garlic
salt and pepper
8 bay leaves, plus more for decoration
4 fillets of John Dory (or sole or tilapia), each 6-8 ounces

method

Cut the vegetables into ¼-inch dice. Heat 2 tablespoons of the olive oil in a frying pan and brown the fennel, onion and zucchini separately. Combine the vegetables in a casserole and add the garlic, salt and pepper. Leave to cook gently for about 15 minutes.

Meanwhile, slip 2 bay leaves between the skin and the flesh of each fillet of John Dory (or sole or tilapia) and fry in the remaining olive oil for 5 minutes on the skin side and 2 minutes on the other side.

Put some of the vegetables on each plate, place a fillet of John Dory (or sole or tilapia) on top and drizzle with olive oil. Decorate with bay leaves.

Bass with crispy skin, diced vegetables with bay leaves, onion compote and vinaigrette

loup à la peau croustillante
mirepoix de légumes au laurier, compote d'oignons et vinaigrette à l'huile d'olive

ingredients

2 thick fillets of loup or grouper
 (with the skin left on), each 6-8 ounces
4 bay twigs, to serve
4 bay leaves, to garnish
7 ounces balsamic vinegar, reduced to a syrup,
 to serve

for the onion compote

8 onions, finely chopped
7 ounces smoked slab bacon, rind removed and
 finely chopped
2 tablespoons olive oil

for the vinaigrette

1 tablespoon balsamic vinegar
3 tablespoons olive oil
salt and pepper

for the mirepoix

½ red bell pepper
½ green bell pepper
3 ounces celery root
½ zucchini
1 tomato
2 tablespoons olive oil
⅓ cup black olives, pitted and chopped
1 pinch of saffron
1½ tablespoons capers
½ tablespoon crushed garlic
2 dried bay leaves, pulverized
salt and pepper

method

To make the onion compote, cook the onions and bacon in the olive oil until soft. To make the mirepoix, dice the vegetables and fry gently in the olive oil with the olives, saffron, capers, garlic, bay leaves, salt and pepper until tender.

Remove the skin from the fish and dry it out in a warm oven, 220°F. Halve each fish fillet and steam the 4 pieces until tender, about 15 minutes.

Prepare the vinaigrette by mixing all the ingredients together.

Place some of the onion compote on each plate. Arrange a fish fillet alongside, cover with the mirepoix, and place a piece of crispy skin on the top like a sail (using a bay twig as a mast). Drizzle the vinaigrette over and decorate with a bay leaf and the reduced balsamic vinegar.

Confit of rabbit shoulder in olive oil and roast saddle of rabbit, blinis with bay leaves and eggplant compote

épaule de lapin confite dans l'huile d'olive, râble rôti
blinis au laurier et compote d'aubergines

Although rabbit is considered to be a peasant dish, it is favored by many top chefs and appears often on the menu in Provence restaurants. Wild rabbit has a better, more gamy flavor, but farmed rabbit is more tender.

ingredients

	for the blinis	for the eggplant compote
2 rabbits, each 1¾-2 pounds, jointed	¾ cup plus 2 tablespoons milk	4 medium eggplants
1 quart olive oil	4 bay leaves	salt and pepper
1 bunch of flat-leaf parsley, chopped	1 cake (⅖ ounce) compressed fresh yeast	olive oil
5 ounces caul-fat		juice of 1 lemon
1 onion, chopped	1½ cups all-purpose flour	
3 cloves of garlic	3 eggs, separated	
small bay leaves, to garnish	butter or oil	

method

To make the eggplant compote, prick the eggplants all over and cook in a hot oven for 1 hour. Remove, halve and scoop out the flesh into a colander. Leave to drain, then sprinkle with salt and pepper, some olive oil and a little lemon juice.

Season the shoulders of rabbit with salt and pepper and brown them in a little of the olive oil, then add most of the remaining olive oil and bake in a low oven for 1 hour. Meanwhile, bone the saddles of rabbit. Season with salt and pepper and sprinkle with parsley. Roll each saddle up and wrap in caul-fat. Freeze the rabbit thighs to use in another recipe. Brown the saddles in a casserole in a little olive oil with the onion, garlic and bay leaves. Moisten with ⅔ cup of water and bake in the oven until the rabbit is tender.

To make the blinis, warm the milk in a small saucepan and add the bay leaves. Leave to infuse for 30 minutes, then strain. Mix together the yeast, ⅓ cup of the flour and the milk, and leave to rise for 1 hour, then add the rest of the flour and the 3 egg yolks. Beat the egg whites until stiff and fold in. Season to taste with salt and pepper. Cook the blinis in a little butter or oil in a frying pan.

On each plate, place 1 shoulder of rabbit, half a saddle, 2 blinis and a portion of eggplant compote. Boil the liquid in the casserole to reduce, then pour over the rabbit. Garnish with bay leaves.

Bay leaf sorbet

sorbet au laurier

This recipe demonstrates the versatility of bay leaves, which are too often confined to savory dishes. Serve the sorbet just before the dessert course.

ingredients

1 cup sugar
juice of 1 lemon
4 bay leaves, plus extra to decorate

method

Put the sugar and lemon juice in a saucepan and add 2¼ cups water. Bring to the boil, then add the bay leaves. Remove the saucepan from the heat, cover with a lid and leave to infuse for 30 minutes.

Pass the contents through a strainer and leave until cold.

Pour into an ice-cream maker and churn for 30 minutes. Store in the freezer, removing 15 minutes before serving, decorated with bay leaves.

the herb
sage
at la bastide de moustiers

Sage, *Salvia officinalis*, is one of nature's great healing plants. The very name "salvia" derives from the Latin *salvare*, meaning "to save" or "to cure." In ancient Egypt and in Rome it was looked upon as a sacred plant and treated with great reverence. The Romans even went so far as to ceremonially offer a sacrifice of bread and wine to the gods before gathering sage, barefoot, dressed in white tunics, and avoiding the use of iron cutting tools. Considered to be a life-enhancing herb and an aid to good health, in France it was given the name "Toute-Bonne," and Vincent Maillard, the chef at La Bastide, tells me there is a saying which goes, "How can a man die who has sage in his garden?" There was even a belief among the Gauls that sage could resuscitate the dead.

In the kitchen garden at La Bastide there are three types of sage: green sage (*Salvia officinalis*), purple, sometimes called red, sage (*Salvia purpurea*) and clary sage (*Salvia sclarea*). These are the most commonly used in cooking and grow well in this region, having replaced the wild sage that used to grow in abundance in southern Europe. These cultivated forms have the same properties and virtues as the wild sage and can be easily grown for use in the kitchen and home.

Sage can be gathered all the year round in Provence providing the winters are mild. However, at La Bastide de Moustiers they take the precaution of drying some leaves in the early autumn. The winter months can be unpredictable.

It is important to remember sage is a strong herb. In cooking always use it sparingly. In this case it is

well to follow the adage, "less is more." A meal can very easily be spoilt by introducing too much of the herb in the misguided belief that because it is so health-giving, the more you use, the better it is for you. Do not be tempted to over-indulge yourself. In character sage is a selfish herb, wanting to dominate the stage. It is, I am told, "an easily offended and capricious prima donna."

cultivation

Most sages grow to a height of between 18 and 24 inches, but clary sage has been known to grow as high as 3 feet. They are classed as evergreens. Sage grows best in a dry stony soil with good drainage and can be propagated from seed or by taking cuttings from young shoots in the spring, when it will take readily in potting compost with the addition of sharp sand. Old woody bushes can be mounded up with surrounding earth in the autumn, to produce new shoots in the following year. The leaves are ovate and velvety to the touch, with a strong aroma. Flowers appear from late spring until mid-summer and are a purplish blue color on *Salvia officinalis* and a pale lilac-white on clary sage.

culinary uses

Sage is an excellent digestif and can also be taken before meals to aid the digestion. A much more versatile herb than is often imagined, it is associated with stuffings for meat, but is also excellent with some fish, such as eel, when the leaves are wrapped around it. It can be added to cheese in omelettes, or in a cheese spread; in meat sauces and stews of all kinds. Young leaves are infused with elderflowers to give a muscatel aroma to Alsace wines.

the restaurant
la bastide de moustiers

It is late spring in Alpes-de-Haute-Provence. The early morning mist fills the valley below the ancient town of Moustiers Sainte-Marie, little changed since the late seventeenth century when it was the center for the world famous faïence pottery industry. La Bastide de Moustiers was the home of a master faïence maker and now, having been lovingly restored by Alain Ducasse, is a comfortable country retreat for this most eminent of French chefs. It is easy to imagine his love affair with this tranquil place, chosen as a spiritual center by Christian monks as far back as the Crusades. The first thing you notice is the silence, broken only by the sound of dripping leaves as the Provençal sun rises over the rugged, honey-colored escarpment above the town and instantly thaws out the early frost. The general sense of well-being is enhanced by the clearance of the mist, revealing a field of neatly clipped lavender below giving promise of the summer to come.

La Bastide is deceptively large inside without losing its intimacy. It is like visiting the home of a friend and I am intrigued to know where the kitchen is. It comes as even more of a surprise to find it unchanged from its original size, neatly tucked away at one corner of the building. A brigade of just five men are quietly preparing the meal of the day. The room resembles the kitchen of a sophisticated farmhouse, with a central preparation table above which hangs an assortment of gleaming copper saucepans and utensils. There are sinks at one side, ovens and grills on the other and an antique rotisserie in the corner. Watching them work under the guidance of M. Vincent Maillard, I am fascinated by their almost telepathic understanding of each other's space.

Outside the kitchen door is a terrace leading to the potager garden containing cultivated herbs and vegetables for La Bastide. Elsewhere, wherever there is a bank or border, herbs such as thyme, rosemary and lavender are growing. For M. Ducasse the use of herbs is essential to the Provençal cuisine. His emphasis is on traditional rustic food which at the same time is refined. The balance is crucial and the love of the local produce makes it possible.

I am enchanted by the dining-rooms. Three rooms lead on one from the other within a few paces of the kitchen. The low plaster ceilings allow for an intimate setting, enhanced by the antique walnut chimney-piece with an open fire in the grate in the main room. The other two smaller rooms are the Salon des Faïenciers, with three dining tables and decorated with examples of local ateliers' work within, and the aptly named Salon des Amoureux, with just one table taking up the entire room for the quintessential intimate dinner for two. The small library room situated behind the fireplace has a number of personal treasures in cabinets between the bookshelves, adding to the feeling that you are sharing in someone else's collection of memorabilia. Something about Provence allows you to be part of people's lives. The welcome is very human and sincere.

the chef
vincent maillard

M. Maillard, the chef de cuisine at La Bastide de Moustiers, is only in his twenty-fifth year. But it is a testament to the faith that Alain Ducasse has in him that after only two years working in Monaco, at the Louis XV hotel, M. Maillard was given the opportunity to extend his talents here at Moustiers. M. Ducasse's philosophy for the kitchen is: "Tasting a dish must be a memorable event. If not a single guest remembers anything about it, I've got it wrong." Vincent Maillard has taken this to heart and with quiet efficiency he goes about creating dishes to stick in your memory. He tells me, "From day to day I look at what is in the garden and make a menu. No set routine for me." Each and every day Vincent Maillard goes out to the potager garden and chooses vegetables and herbs that are at their best and from them creates a menu for that particular day. The beauty of this philosophy is that you are spared the business of choosing your meal. It is chosen for you.

Since leaving school at the tender age of fourteen – something the young people of France are encouraged to do if they have a strong vocation – M. Maillard went from his home town of Beaune, in Burgundy, to study cookery at Le Touquet, a town on the north coast. After completing his National Service in 1993 he made for Provence, and in particular the Côte d'Azur. He will celebrate his twenty-fifth birthday working as chef at La Bastide and is in no hurry to move on.

When I first met him he had only been in charge for a matter of months but already he had the respect and confidence of his small brigade. To watch him preparing the early spring vegetables with quick concentrated movements, head bent over the chopping board cutting and discarding, to achieve the best effect from uneven material, it is easy to see why. He has all the attributes of an artist without the explosive temperament. They are all young and energetic in the brigade and go about their daily tasks with controlled gusto. The kitchen is always open to guests, who can visit it as if it were their own. This valley below the town has a fertile soil – monastic orders knew a good productive site when they saw one – and the combination of Vincent Maillard's quiet devotion to his art and the history of this region makes for a perfect spirituality of cuisine. After tasting the fresh young asparagus, the first of the season, I can only envy M. Maillard his own little corner of paradise.

"Leave the common herd behind you
and approach everything in a new way."

Geometry of pasta scented with sage and green and white Provençal asparagus

géométrie de pâtes parfumées à la sauge
asperges vertes et blanches de provence

From the moment I first saw this dish prepared by Vincent Maillard it reminded me of those early Renaissance paintings of "The Veil of Veronica." The artistry of the chef involved great delicacy in the preparation of the pasta and in placing it upon the asparagus. You will need to serve this almost immediately to avoid the misery of the pasta drying out and splitting open.

ingredients

	for the green pasta	**for the white pasta**
12 spears of green asparagus	1½ cups all-purpose flour	1½ cups all-purpose flour
8 spears of white asparagus	½ cup puréed spinach	
8 sage leaves	1 egg	salt
a little chicken or vegetable stock		2 eggs
1 tablespoon olive oil		

method

Break off the tough ends of the asparagus spears and tie the spears together in 2 bunches. Bring a large saucepan of water to the boil and blanch the asparagus for 5 minutes. Drain and cool. Remove the string.

To make the green pasta, put the flour and puréed spinach into a processor, then add the egg. Pulse blend until the pasta comes together into a loose ball of dough. Knead until smooth and elastic. This takes about 15 minutes. Wrap in plastic wrap and leave to rest in a cool place for 2 hours.

To make the white pasta, put the flour and salt into a processor. Add the eggs. Pulse blend until the pasta comes together into a loose ball of dough. Knead until smooth and elastic. This also takes about 15 minutes. Wrap in plastic wrap and leave to rest in a cool place for 2 hours.

Roll one small piece of the dough out at a time until paper thin. Cut out 2 shapes and press a sage leaf between them, using either a rolling pin or a pasta machine. Do this 3 more times. Lightly dust with flour. In a large saucepan cook the pasta in a generous amount of salted, boiling water until al dente, then drain it.

Warm the asparagus in a little stock with the olive oil and 4 sage leaves and arrange on the plate with the pasta.

Mille-feuille of chard, ricotta and sage gnocchi, with bacon

mille-feuille de côte à vert de blettes
gnocchi de lait caillé à la sauge et lard paysau

Provençal gnocchi are little dumplings that can be flavored with herbs and make for a delightful addition to a main dish.

ingredients

1 bunch of chard

olive oil

3½ ounces streaky smoked slab bacon, rind removed

a little vegetable stock flavored with sage

beef jus

for the gnocchi

7 ounces ricotta cheese

2⅔ tablespoons all-purpose flour

1 egg

3 sage leaves, roughly chopped

method

Preheat the oven to 400°F.

To make the gnocchi, place a large pan of salted water on the heat and bring to simmering point. Combine the ricotta, flour, egg and sage leaves and mix thoroughly. Form the mixture into quenelle (dumpling) shapes using 2 teaspoons and place in the simmering water, a few at a time. Poach carefully until the gnocchi rise to the surface – approximately 2 minutes. Remove from the pan with a slotted spoon.

Cut the stalks from the chard leaves and remove any strings running lengthwise with a peeler. Stir-fry the green leaves in olive oil on a high heat until tender and steam the white stalks for about 8 minutes. Cut the stalks into rectangles. While the chard stalks are steaming, cut the bacon into strips, place on a baking tray and put into the preheated oven for a few minutes, or until pale brown.

Arrange the green leaves and white stalks in a serving dish in alternate layers (mille-feuille) and keep warm. Warm the gnocchi in a little stock flavored with sage.

Surround the mille-feuille with the gnocchi, each garnished with a piece of bacon, and drizzle a little beef jus around it.

Tomato, sage and goat's cheese tartlet with arugula salad

tartelette à la tomate et caille doux
à la sauge de roquette

Caille Doux is a curd cheese made from goat's milk. The milk is fermented and allowed to partially dry out. It is a fresh soft cheese which is most often eaten soon after it has drained, but it can be allowed to mature when it will develop a gray crust, giving it the appearance of a pebble, from which it gets its name.

ingredients

for the tartlet pastry dough

1^2/$_3$ cups all-purpose flour

5 tablespoons water

1 tablespoon olive oil

1 egg

for the salad

2 tablespoons balsamic vinegar

5 tablespoons olive oil

7 ounces arugula

for the filling

2 pounds tomatoes

olive oil

3 cloves of garlic, chopped

1 sprig of thyme

2 bay leaves

1 or 2 leaves of sage, finely chopped

7 ounces Caille Doux or any soft goat's cheese

method

To make the pastry, strain the flour into a large bowl. Add the water, oil and egg and mix with a palette knife to form a soft dough. Leave to rest for 2 hours.

Preheat the oven to 220°F. To make the filling, skin the tomatoes by plunging them into boiling water for 15 seconds. Remove the seeds and slice the flesh into petal shapes (quartered but thin). Arrange on an oiled baking sheet, sprinkle with olive oil, garlic, thyme and bay leaves and bake in the preheated oven for 3 hours (do take the trouble to do this, it makes all the difference). Remove the tomatoes, then turn the oven up to 350°F.

Roll out the pastry very thinly, stamp out circles using a 2½-inch cookie cutter and line individual tartlet tins. Bake in the oven for 5 minutes, then remove and cool. Mix the sage with the cheese, reserving a little for decoration. Spread on to the pastry and cover with the tomatoes.

For the salad, make a vinaigrette with the balsamic vinegar and olive oil. Dress the arugula with the vinaigrette. Place a tartlet on each plate and decorate with the reserved cheese. Drizzle vinaigrette on to the plate, then place the salad to the side.

Braised Mediterranean bass with lemon and sage, fennel, cebettes and black olives

loup de méditerranée
braisé au citron et à la sauge, fenouil, fondant cebette et olive taggiashe

This is a delicious variation on the traditional Provençal recipe of bass cooked on a bed of fennel stalks. This beautiful silver fish has also been called "loup de mer," which translated literally means "sea wolf."

ingredients

1 bass or grouper, 3 pounds
2 fennel bulbs
8 cebettes (Provençal baby leeks) or scallions
olive oil
about ⅔ cup vegetable stock
⅔ cup black olives, pitted
salt and pepper
1 lemon, finely sliced
4 sage leaves
young fennel stalks to garnish

method

Preheat the oven to 475°F. Clean and scale the bass.

Trim the fennel bulbs, removing any tough outer leaves and cut in half. Put them in a large pan of boiling water, bring to the boil again and blanch for 6 minutes. Drain, then transfer to another pan, add the cebettes and brown gently in olive oil before adding the stock. Bring to simmering point, cover and cook for 45 minutes or until tender. Add the olives.

To cook the fish, brush it inside and out with a little olive oil, then season inside and out with salt and pepper. Place in a roasting dish, cover the fish with fine slices of lemon, the sage leaves and about 6 tablespoons of stock. Cook in the preheated oven for 20 minutes, basting a couple of times with the juices from the tray.

Remove from the oven. Place the fish on a bed of fennel stalks on a serving dish together with the vegetables and olives.

Roast knuckle of milk-fed veal with sage-glazed vegetables

jarret de veau de lait cuisiné au four à la sauge
légumes glacés au jus

If you are unable to obtain fresh baby fava beans, frozen ones will suffice. Canned artichoke hearts can be used instead of fresh. If you feel you want more juice, use 2 glasses of water rather than one.

ingredients

1 knuckle of veal

1 small bunch of sage

10 ounces spinach

2 pounds fevettes (baby fava beans, the first of the season)

8 artichokes

8 carrots with their green tops

7 tablespoons olive oil

dab of butter

toasted croûtons

method

Preheat the oven to 350°F. Trim the veal and rub with a few sage leaves. Roast in the preheated oven for about 50 minutes, turning and basting every 5 minutes.

Prepare the vegetables. Clean the spinach. Pod the fevettes. Trim the artichokes of their leaves and remove the chokes. Scrape the carrots. Heat the oil and fry the carrots and artichoke hearts. Cook the spinach in a separate pan with a dab of butter.

Once the veal is cooked, take it out of the oven. Put it in a warmed ovenproof dish and leave it to stand for 30 minutes. Deglaze the roasting pan with a glass of water, stirring the sticky bits from the bottom of the pan. Strain the resulting sauce into a serving dish and add the rest of the sage.

Remove the marrow from the veal bone and spread it on toasted croûtons. Return the veal and the vegetables to the sauce. Baste. Serve the veal surrounded by the vegetables and the croûtons.

Roast pigeon with sage and spring vegetables

pigeonneau contisé de sauge et rôti en cocotte
légumes de printemps

We have Elizabeth David to thank for introducing us to the "plump and tender little creatures of the *volière*, or pigeon run," bred for the pot. These are treated more like game birds than poultry and are best cooked when young but fully grown. If you are unable to buy young pigeon, then you must be prepared to cook them for up to 40 minutes longer. This is a true springtime recipe.

ingredients

4 pigeons, 1 pound each
4 sage leaves
7 tablespoons olive oil
2 pounds petits peas
4 scallions, halved lengthwise if large
1 bulb of new season garlic, cloves separated
7 ounces chicken stock
salt and pepper

method

Preheat the oven to 350°F.

Clean and prepare the pigeons. Slide sage leaves under the skin and put the birds in a solid roasting tin or flameproof casserole with their giblets. Pour over 2 tablespoons of the olive oil.

Pod the petits peas and peel the onions and garlic.

Roast the pigeon and giblets in the preheated oven for 20 minutes until cooked and golden brown. Once cooked, remove the pigeons to a hot plate. Pour 7 ounces of water into the pan and cook gently for 10 to 20 minutes to make a delicious syrup. Strain and reserve. Cook the onions and garlic in the remaining olive oil in the casserole dish. Once the onions are soft, add the petit peas. Add the chicken stock plus salt and pepper. As soon as the petit peas are cooked through, return the pigeons to the casserole with the strained pigeon "syrup." Warm through and serve.

Suckling pig larded with sage and cooked on the spit, with fritters, fried and crushed potatoes

cochon de lait à la sauge cuit à la broche
fritot, pommes de terre écrasées à la fourchette

Suckling, or sucking pig, is a young piglet at the weaning stage. It is always cooked whole upon a spit and because of its small size is just about suitable for four persons.

ingredients

1 suckling pig, 3½ pounds in weight
12 sage leaves
6 large red or white potatoes
olive oil
salt and pepper
oil for deep frying
2 thin slices of Jambon de Bayonne, or prosciutto, cut in half

for the niçois pastry
⅓ cup all-purpose flour
5 tablespoons water
1 or 2 eggs
trickle of olive oil

method

Make slits in the skin of the suckling pig. Slice 4 sage leaves and push into the slits. Cook on the spit at 350°F for about 30 minutes or until the meat is tender.

Boil 4 potatoes in their skins, then peel and crush them with a fork, adding olive oil and salt.

Slice the remaining potatoes finely and deep fry in the oil.

Make the pastry by mixing all the ingredients together. Roll it out thinly. Place a half slice of ham between 2 sage leaves, and repeat with the remaining ham and sage leaves. Cover with pastry and deep fry until golden brown.

Serve the meat with the potatoes and pastries and hand the meat juices separately.

the herb
fennel
at chez bruno

All alongside the road from the town of Lorgues to Chez Bruno there are wild fennel plants, *Foeniculum vulgare*. Fennel grows abundantly in the South of France and its fronds of green feathery leaves and umbels of yellow flowers make it easy to recognize in the wild. The leaf stalks in the cultivated form make a sheath around the stout stem, often as far as the base of the leaf above it. Its name derives from the Latin word *foenum* meaning "hay," and it was certainly introduced to Provence by the Romans as a culinary herb. As far back as 1640 the herbalist Parkinson, in his *Theatricum Botanicum* said: "The leaves, seede and rootes are both for meate and medicine; the Italians especially doe much delight in the use thereof, and therefore transplant and whiten it, to make it more tender to please the taste, which being sweete and somewhat hot helpeth to digest the crude qualitie of fish and other viscous meats."

There is no doubt of its carminative effect and this caused it to be a great favorite of Rabelais in some of his humorous texts. However, it was also revered as a protective herb, to be hung with Saint John's Wort over doorways on Midsummer's Eve to ward off evil spirits. The Romans looked upon it as a strength-giving herb and the Greeks called it *marathron*, meaning "to grow thin," since which time it has been used to treat obesity. Pliny was particularly fond of its medicinal properties and gives us an insight into his practical research when he refers to his observation of snakes who ate it, "when they cast their old skins, and sharpen their sight with the juice by rubbing against the plant." In ancient Egypt it was recommended as an antidote to poisons and even today it is recognized as a swift expeller of poison in the blood if a person is bitten by a snake, dog or any other animal.

The Florentine dwarf fennel is an annual, and produces leaves at the base which overlap and form swellings referred to by most cooks as "bulbs." This fennel is a great favorite of the Italians and as a result has found a place in the cuisine of Provence. M. Saugnac, the chef at Chez Bruno, uses fennel leaves, stems and the bulb in the kitchen to great effect.

cultivation

Fennel is not a sociable herb. Growing to a height of between 3 and 4½ feet, it prefers a solitary, open, sunny aspect away from other herbs, in particular cilantro. Seed can be sown early in the spring or the previous autumn in soil that is not too rich but dry. Roots from established plants can be divided in the spring. There are many different varieties but my favorite is bronze fennel (*Foeniculum purpureum*), which looks particularly good as a background plant for golden-leafed shrubs or growing in front of a golden hop. Seeds can be harvested in late summer just before they ripen and dried in a cool, shady place with good air circulation.

culinary uses

Fennel's beneficial effect on the digestion is well documented and, mixed with marjoram and mint, it makes a very refreshing digestif after a meal. The leaves can be chopped up in sauces to impart a rich aniseed flavor and the sprigs added to salads, fish dishes and marinades, while the seeds can be used in hors-d'oeuvre, with eggs and cheese, roast pork, apple pie and on cakes and biscuits. The delicately flavored leaves of Florence fennel go well in salads and the bulbous leaf stem can be eaten raw.

the restaurant
chez bruno

The land surrounding the town of Lorgues in the south-west of Provence is rich farming land and vineyards abound. "Here," the saying goes, "water is gold." The many fountains in the old town are proof of the need for this most precious of commodities, without which the approaching months of intense heat would dry up the land and burn the crops. At Chez Bruno water is everywhere, filtering down from the many terraces above the house and filling up stone basins, where it is pumped through central spouts. Here liquid gold meets black gold – the truffle, that much sought-after fungal delicacy that can enrich a dish with primordial intensity. Discovered among the roots of young oak trees, it used to be harvested by pigs that were trained to snuffle out the black nuggets from the soil, attracted by the smell and keen to compete with their handlers for the prize. Clément Bruno, a giant of a man with generosity of spirit to match, has built his reputation on the cuisine of the truffle and his international clientele arrive here as if on a pilgrimage to the home of the "Truffle Emperor of the Var." M. Bruno has inscribed his welcome at the top of the steps which lead to the restaurant. It says, "*Ici s'arrête la réussite sociale, Mais commence la réussite humaine.*" Quite simply, "Here social success ends, but human success begins." In other words he is here to please us rather than himself.

It is quite something to be welcomed at the entrance to his restaurant by Clément Bruno. The arms are extended outwards as he opens himself to you and a deep guttural cry emanates from his huge frame. "Welcome to my home, come in and enjoy," is the essence of a Bruno welcome. Entering through the oak-studded door into the reception area, the low ceiling has a delightful painting of putti sporting among the clouds with baskets of truffles described by banners, reading – *Tuber brumale, Tuber incinatum, Tuber aestivum*, and others. It offers the sort of delight that makes you smile and the oak-panelled room with molded stone fireplace draws you in, where you are seated in ivory-painted, wooden armchairs at ample-sized tables with room to expand and relax.

Outside on the terrace, wisteria, jasmine and honeysuckle give way to bamboo awnings, allowing the dappled light to fall on to an assortment of tables laid with white linen and surrounded by dark green ironwork chairs. The overall sense is of green: green-leafed young oak trees, pollarded Chinese mulberries, cherry trees and a grassy terraced lawn to look upon. There are quirky ornaments in the kitchens, which are worth seeing – a wooden cockerel with orange-ribboned chef's medal around its neck, cabinets with truffle jars and jars of preserved fruits. The décor is burgundy and cream, with cream and green tiles on the walls. The work surfaces are gray marble and, because these are the old cellars of the house, there are skylights above with painted cherries in the surrounds. In a large dining-room directly off the kitchens a life-size, blown-glass truffle merchant holds enough truffles in his arms to pay off your mortgage. But it is the wall painting of M. Bruno at a vast table laid with every delicacy imaginable that catches the eye. Holding knife and fork, he is watched by a demure little girl standing to one side of the table just waiting to be asked to join him. I can almost hear him declaiming, "*C'est formidable.*"

the chef
dominique saugnac

In the kitchens at Chez Bruno there is an inscription which reads, *"Un travail bien fait m'est plus à faire, faisons le avec le coeur."* "A job well done is not worth doing unless it is done from the heart." M. Bruno encourages team spirit and the team is led by Dominique Saugnac, a vital, enthusiastic worker with impish charm.

M. Saugnac was born in the south-west of France in the tiny village of Carcen-Ponson, in the Landes district. He adapted so well to working, alongside Alain Ducasse, at the fashionable resort of Juan-les-Pins, near Antibes, where he stayed for seven years, that M. Ducasse introduced him to his great friend Clément Bruno, who was looking for just such a partner at Lorgues. After seven years at Chez Bruno I cannot see him wanting to move on in a hurry. His energetic enthusiasm is tempered by M. Bruno's calm control. "M. Bruno is the man with the ideas and I am the one who develops them in a creative way," he tells me. "I am very much in tune with M. Bruno's way of thinking. He is not only my mentor but he has also become a true friend and confidant."

"Our philosophy is guided by our clientele," he explains. "We have great respect for our clients' wishes, offering them an escape from the cares of commerce and providing for their inner needs. Quality, spontaneity, simplicity, respect for the food and for the client. These rules govern us. But creativity is the constant desire."

M. Saugnac thinks quickly and delighted in creating recipes for me in a spontaneous way. An idea would come to him and without any more fuss he would set about creating it, relishing in the amusement it gave him. M. Bruno gave him a free hand and never once interfered with this stream of consciousness. The results, as you can see, are simple yet sophisticated. His talent coupled with his confidence are disarming. What was even more alarming at first was when I asked him for the written recipes. " I don't have them," he said with a smile, "they are all here," pointing to his head. We quickly wrote down all the titles, and left them with him. I need not have worried. A few weeks later they arrived on my fax machine, with a delightful message addressed to "Cher Ami." I should think Dominique Saugnac makes friends easily.

"Quality, spontaneity, simplicity,
respect for the food and for the client."

Salad of raw fennel, Parmesan and truffles with olive oil

la salade de fenouil cru, parmesan et truffes
à l'huile d'olive

Take care to grate the truffle very thinly. Apart from the expense, the flavor can be too intense and overpower the other tastes.

ingredients

2 large bulbs of early fennel

¾ cup plus 2 tablespoons olive oil

1 good head of iceberg lettuce

7 ounces arugula

5½ ounces aged Parmesan cheese

4 ounces summer truffles (or truffle shavings)

method

Cut the fennel bulbs into very thin slices and put them in a bowl. Pour the olive oil over and leave to marinate for 6 hours.

Wash the salad leaves and drain in a colander, then spread on a flat plate. Place the fennel on top of the salad leaves. Add shavings of Parmesan and thin slices of truffle and drizzle with olive oil.

Iced cream of fennel soup, summer truffles and olive oil

le velouté glacé de fenouil
aux truffes d'été et huile d'olive

A truffle is known in Provence as a *rabasse*, after the legend concerning an old woman by the name of La Rabasse, who was given the secret of truffle cultivation by a bird that she rescued. Those who hunt the truffle are known as *rabasseurs*.

ingredients

4 green fennel bulbs
2¼ cups strong chicken stock
¾ cup plus 2 tablespoons olive oil

1 cup whipping cream
a few slices of summer truffles (or truffle
   shavings)

method

Cut the fennel into large pieces. Blanch in salted water. Refresh in cold water and drain.

Place the chicken stock, olive oil, cream and fennel in a food processor or blender. Liquefy for 4 to 5 minutes. Pass through a fine strainer, then chill.

Just before serving, add a few slices of summer truffles (do not overdo this).

Gratin of young fennel with anchovies and olives

le gratin de jeunes fenouils aux anchois et olives

This deceptively simple dish makes perfect use of young fennel, and croûtons with tomato or olive paste make a delicious accompaniment.

ingredients

1⅓ tablespoons butter

2⅔ tablespoons all-purpose flour

2¼ cups milk

1½ pounds young fennel bulbs and stalks

5½ ounces anchovies in oil

1½ cups black kalamata or niçois olives

½ cup grated Parmesan cheese

method

Preheat the oven to 375°F.

Melt the butter in a saucepan over a low heat and stir in the flour. Add the milk gradually, to make a béchamel sauce.

Blanch the young fennel and drain. Place in a gratin dish. Criss-cross the anchovies on top and add the olives. Pour over the béchamel sauce, sprinkle with Parmesan cheese and bake in the preheated oven for approximately 20 minutes or until brown on top.

Tempura of fennel tops and bulbs with sun-dried tomatoes with basil and tapenade

la tempura de fenouil fane et bulbe
– tomate confite au basilic – et tapenade

The addition of sun-dried tomatoes with basil and tapenade makes this a truly Provençal dish. Tapenade, a paste made with capers, or *tapena*, and olives is easily available in good delicatessens.

ingredients

2 fennel bulbs with feathery tops
10 ounces sun-dried tomatoes in olive oil
4 basil leaves
4 tablespoons tapenade

for the tempura batter
1 cup potato flour (fécule)
¾ cup plus 1½ tablespoons all-purpose flour
1 cake (⅗ ounce) compressed fresh yeast
1¾ cups very cold water
oil for deep frying

method

Slice the fennel bulbs finely, lengthwise. Keep the feathery tops to one side.

Chop the tomatoes and basil and mix together.

To make the tempura batter, mix together the two flours, yeast and water in a large bowl. Heat deep frying oil to a temperature of 350°F.

Dip fennel tops and slices into the tempura batter. Deep fry, then drain on a cloth or kitchen paper.

Arrange on 4 plates – half fennel, half fennel tops. Make a little heap of tomatoes with basil, and one of tapenade, on each plate.

River trout "en papillote" with fennel and white wine

la truite de rivière cuite en papillote
au fenouil et vin blanc

This is a variation on a Provençal theme, where bass is flamed over a fire of dried fennel stalks. The fennel stalks need to be dried over a number of days in an airy room, out of the sun.

ingredients

2 shallots

1 clove of garlic

fennel leaves and dried stems

¾ cup plus 2 tablespoons white wine

1 tablespoon olive oil

4 trout, about 8 ounces each, scaled and cleaned

1 lemon

1 branch of thyme

salt and pepper

for the beurre blanc sauce

2 shallots, finely chopped

7 ounces white wine

7 tablespoons butter

juice of ½ lemon

method

Preheat the oven to 425°F.

Chop the shallots, garlic and fennel leaves very finely. Put in a bowl and add the white wine and the olive oil. Leave to marinate for 15 minutes, then drain, reserving the marinade.

Take 4 pieces of greaseproof paper or foil, each 12 x 8 inches, and divide the marinated fennel and shallots between them. Add 1 trout, covered with 2 slices of lemon and some thyme leaves. Pour the marinade juices over and add salt and pepper to taste. Seal the packages very carefully.

Cook in the preheated oven for 12 minutes on a bed of fennel stems.

To make the beurre blanc sauce, put the shallots and white wine in a small pan and reduce to half over high heat. Away from the flame, add the butter and stir till melted, then add a little lemon juice.

Serve the fish as soon as it is cooked, handing the sauce separately.

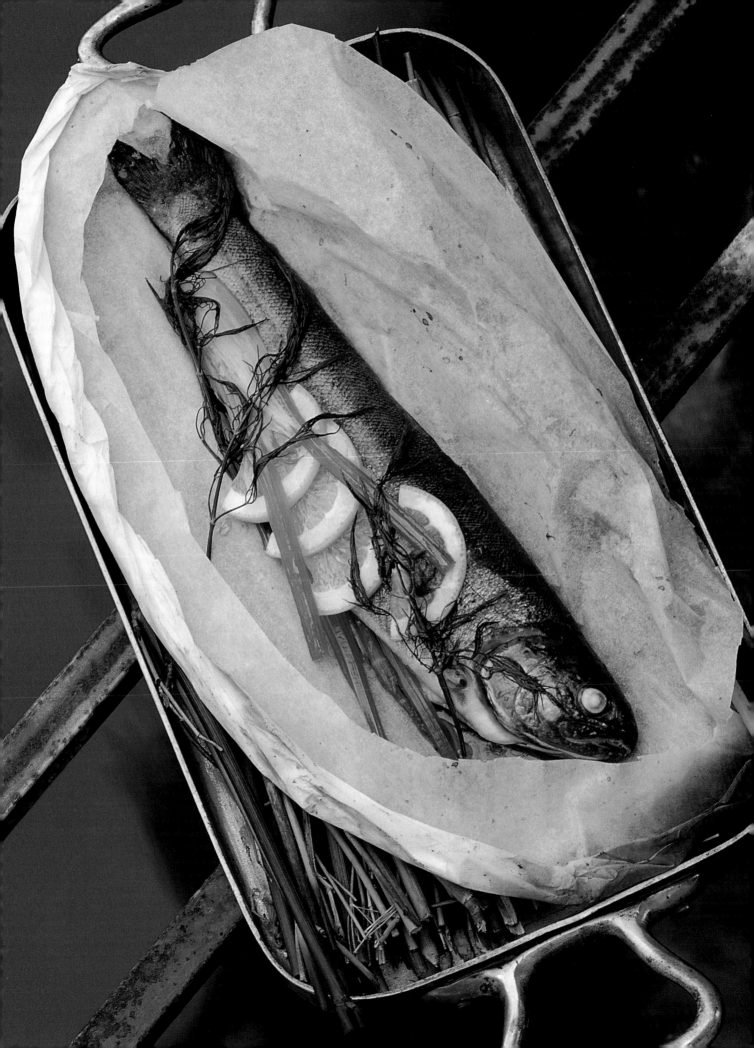

Fennel confit with red fruits and star anise syrup

le fenouil confit aux fruits rouges
sirop à l'anis étoilé

Star anise, or Chinese anise, is a star-shaped fruit from a small evergreen tree in China. Each point of the star contains a small shiny brown seed. The flavor is similar to anise, used to flavor the alcoholic drink *pastis*.

ingredients

1 fennel bulb
½ cup plus 2 tablespoons sugar
1 cup water
4 to 5 star anise
4 vanilla beans
strawberries and raspberries for decoration

method

Separate the fennel stems. Dissolve the sugar in the water, add 3 or 4 star anise and the vanilla beans, then add the fennel and simmer until it is translucent. Remove the fennel and drain, reserving the syrup.

Cut the fennel into thick batons and place on a plate. Decorate with strawberries and raspberries.

Boil the syrup until reduced and thickened. Trickle a thin line of syrup over the fennel and fruit. Decorate each plate with a vanilla bean.

Sorbet with fennel and pastis

le sorbet au fenouil et pastis

To make the sugared fennel leaf, boil sugar and water together in a saucepan. Remove from the heat before it begins to caramelize and dip the fronds of fennel in the syrup. Leave to set on a sheet of baking parchment.

ingredients

1 fennel bulb plus fennel leaves
½ cup plus 2 tablespoons sugar
2 cups water
3 tablespoons pastis

method

Separate the fennel stems from around the bulb. Dissolve the sugar in 1 cup of the water, add the fennel and simmer until it is translucent.

Add the remaining 1 cup water, pour into a blender and blend until smooth. Add the pastis and pass through a fine strainer. Transfer the mixture to an ice-cream maker and churn for 30 minutes. Store in the freezer, removing 15 minutes before serving.

Decorate with sugared fennel leaf. Plate decoration of fennel and vanilla beans is optional.

the herb
marjoram

at la bastide saint-antoine

There is a popular misconception that oregano is in a class of its own, bearing no relationship to marjoram. Whereas, in fact, oregano is really wild marjoram. Marjoram, *Origanum vulgare*, is the herb found growing on the warm hillsides of Provence. The name "oregano" derives from two words in Greek meaning "joy of the mountains" and it has a cheerful history. Associated with weddings and bridal bouquets, it has an equal place in departures from this life, being planted on graves as a fond farewell. In France marjoram translates as *marjolaine* and appears in a nursery rhyme being given as a gift by a young prince, not singly but as a bouquet. It is well thought of as a panacea, probably due to its sedative properties.

"Marjoram is a summer herb," M. Chibois, the chef at La Bastide, tells me, "it is no good in the winter." Unlike thyme, which can be used all the year, marjoram has a softer leaf and only thrives during the summer months, dying back to the ground where it cowers until the warmth of the spring sun reawakens it. For M. Chibois it is a vivacious herb, good for the digestion and therefore good in food. However, he warns, it is also a powerful herb and should be used in moderation so as not to overpower the tastebuds.

In all my reading about marjoram I have found so much comfort in its reputation. It seems that in the Middle Ages, in France, it was the custom for housewives to plant marjoram in a wooden box of herbs under their windows. This forerunner of today's window-boxes (now mostly filled with pelargoniums) seems to have been a very sensible practice born out of the many uses marjoram had in the home and kitchen. One of the soothing effects it is supposed to have is as a

remedy for headaches and head colds. M. Jean Palaiseul, in his delightful book, *Grandmother's Secrets*, recounts a tale from history: during the Thirty Years War, a famous German physician-surgeon, called Fabricus von Hilden, used marjoram to cure one of his generals, a wealthy statesman called Wallenstein, of a severe head cold. The man was so delighted that he rewarded von Hilden with 200 gold crowns and sent him home to Rostock in his own carriage under military escort.

cultivation

The simplest form of marjoram for cultivation is that known as sweet marjoram, and there is a very pretty form, early in the year, called gold-tipped marjoram, growing in low cushions of leaf. It is a perennial needing full sun and a dry soil. Both wild marjoram and sweet marjoram can be grown from seed in situ in the autumn, but the best form of propagation is from root division in late winter and in the autumn. Cuttings take well in spring and early summer. Sweet marjoram is a more compact plant, but wild marjoram grows to a height of 24 inches with aromatic leaves and pinky mauvish flowers. Harvest the flowers during late summer for drying.

culinary uses

An infusion of marjoram is a beautifully flavored tea with good digestive qualities. Marjoram is delicious as a flavoring for oil or vinegars which can be used for toppings on pizza, tomatoes or broiled fish and pasta. A delicate herb, marjoram is looked upon as an aromatic flavoring for stuffings of all kinds and for sausages. But its versatility is now becoming more apparent, being used in tomato juice cocktails, soups and sauces, with all types of roasting meats and rubbed inside and out of poultry and game.

the restaurant
la bastide saint-antoine

A niche at the west door, protected by glass, contains a statue of St-Antoine of Padua cradling the infant Jesus, clutching a bunch of lilies. This seems highly appropriate, as here at La Bastide Saint-Antoine you are surrounded by terraces of flowers and shrubs. Passion flower, bougainvillea, iris, rosemary, lavender, bay trees clipped into umbrella shapes, oleander and olive trees, at every level of the south-sloping terraces, lead the eye towards the distant view of the sea at Théoule-sur-Mer, twelve miles away. This is the view that Joseph Taylor, the renowned gardener and landscaper from Chicago, would have seen when, in the early nineteenth century, he fell in love with La Bastide and settled here, after being summoned by Lord Brougham to create a garden at Cannes. Then it had 865 acres of land attached to it, and although today the surrounding land is much reduced, it still feels as if you are in the country. Built in the eighteenth century, the perfect proportions of La Bastide and the lush, terraced lawns give it a sense of timeless refinement.

You arrive at the entrance gates with the crowded town of Grasse behind. Scented plants line the drive, prostrate rosemary, shrub roses, white oleanders and gray-leafed perovskia on either side and an olive grove to your right. Through the vine-covered iron pergola, to the left of the soft ocher yellow façade surrounding the entrance to La Bastide, is a gate leading to stairs that take you down to the herb garden below. Here the marjoram is grown for the kitchen, beneath the light shade of an orange tree, whose branches are heavy with summer fruit. The kitchen is large and airy, facing east, giving tantalizing views of the world outside.

This morning waiters are carrying the glass-topped tables into their positions outside for luncheon in the shade of an enormous horse chestnut tree. It is early September and still comfortably warm. The air has been moistened by the lawn sprinklers and the sun shines brightly on the house, which appears little changed in over 200 years. All the technology, which has taken our comfortable existence into the twenty-first century, is carefully concealed indoors and the skyline is not marred by any aerials or satellite dishes. Three colors dominate: soft yellow walls, gray shutters and the bold purple of the bougainvillea which surrounds the open windows.

M. Chibois has taken great care in creating a welcoming feel to La Bastide. Inside the house the low-plastered ceilings disguise the massive timbers that support the rooms above. In the process of restoration M. Chibois has retained the intimacy of the dining areas and introduced an old-fashioned smoking room. Large Provençal fireplaces will be ablaze with logs in the winter months and the soft, gray-green, trompe l'oeil painted panels on the walls together with the floor-length, cream and white tablecloths and rich Chinese rugs will go to make the comfort complete. Looking out through the narrow French windows your eyes are deceived for a moment by three statues of *jeunes filles* on the lawn. Their life-like attitudes are delightfully gauche, adding gentle humor to this elegant setting.

the chef
jacques chibois

For Jacques Chibois, acquiring La Bastide Saint-Antoine was the culmination of a lifetime's dream. Having built an international reputation at the hotel Gray d'Albion in Cannes after elevating its restaurant, the Royal Gray, to two star Michelin status, he was ready to create his own restaurant, with his own unique style of cuisine. There is a lightness of touch, and a taste to his food, that sets him apart from others. This has come from a number of influences on his life. The first of these was his mother, who guided him away from a life in agriculture to lead him into a cooking apprenticeship at a hotel near to his home in Limoges. It was not long before he discovered his vocation and undertook to work on a grueling "*tour de France*" alongside great chefs such as Jean Delavayne, Roger Vergé and Louis Outhier before meeting the strongest influence on his career, Michel Guérard, with whom he worked for five years. During military service he was snapped up by a top general and gained his first award as "Maréchal Chef de Logis."

He was only twenty-nine years old when he took over the Royal Gray restaurant in 1981. In the years that followed he grew to love the Côte d'Azur and began to discover the healthy goodness of the Provençal produce. He refers to the delicacy, personality and structure of a dish. "After cuisine then health is the essence," he tells me. "I learnt to cook according to the dictates of dieticians and herbalists and from this I am able to maintain lightness."

He is passionate about good-quality produce and still manages to maintain his interest in horticulture by growing herbs and some produce on the land surrounding his beloved Bastide. Like so many of the chefs I have encountered in Provence, M. Chibois has a kind, gentle nature and it intrigued me how he manages to maintain this equilibrium. He views the running of the kitchen as a military operation, something I had heard before, but then he said something that clarified the image of his authority so precisely: "There is an artistic feeling to the atmosphere of a kitchen. It is like an orchestra. Each instrument has its work to do. There are leaders of each section and there are others who augment the music. Everyone contributes to the whole, and the whole is brought to its conclusion by me, the conductor. They look to the conductor for guidance and control. I have respect towards my colleagues, but the audience comes first. I transmit this passion to the table. Enjoying food is a moment of happiness." Enjoying M. Chibois' food is a moment of happiness that lingers well after the performance.

"I learnt to cook according to the dictates
of dieticians and herbalists..."

Cold soup of potatoes and tomatoes with marjoram

fraîcheur de pommes de terre et tomates
et pétales de feuilles de marjolaine

This is a perfect way to make the most of the first cherry tomatoes of the season.

ingredients

1 pound white potatoes

2 garlic cloves

10 sage leaves

5 marjoram leaves

4 tablespoons olive oil

7 tablespoons light cream

salt and pepper

a little lemon juice

11 ounces cherry tomatoes

marjoram leaves, to decorate

a few petals of marjoram and jasmine flowers, or rose leaves, for decoration

method

Peel the potatoes and garlic cloves and quarter them. Bring 1 quart water to the boil in a large pan, add the potatoes, garlic, sage and marjoram and cook on a gentle heat for 30 minutes.

Put the contents of the pan into a blender with 3 tablespoons of the olive oil, the cream, salt, pepper and a few drops of lemon juice, and liquefy.

Cut 4 ounces of the cherry tomatoes into quarters, put in a small pan and cook over a high heat for 2 to 3 minutes. Press through a strainer to extract the juice and the pulp. Add salt and pepper and the remaining olive oil. Leave the soup and tomato sauce to chill in the refrigerator.

Serve the soup, sprinkled with marjoram leaves, in a shallow plate and trickle a thin ribbon of the tomato sauce round the edge. Decorate the plate with cherry tomatoes and flowers.

Sautéed vegetables with marjoram as we like them in Provence

le sauté de légumes à la marjolaine
comment on l'aime en provence

Close your eyes and think of Provence.

ingredients

2 large artichokes

2 fennel bulbs

½ red bell pepper

½ yellow bell pepper

1 tomato

10 ounces snow peas

⅔ cup peeled fava beans

1 small onion

6 tablespoons olive oil

2 garlic cloves, peeled

20 very small carrots, with their tops
   (or 20 carrot sticks 3 to 3½ inches long,
   cut from large carrots)

1 tablespoon dried fennel seeds

2 sprigs of marjoram

salt and pepper

juice of ½ lemon

8 basil leaves, finely chopped

method

Prepare the artichokes by removing all the leaves with a knife, and scraping out the choke. Cut each artichoke heart into quarters. Cut the fennel bulbs in half. Cut the bell peppers into ½-inch dice. Peel the tomato, remove the seeds and cut into ½-inch dice. Top and tail the snow peas. Cook the peas in boiling, salted water for 2 to 3 minutes until tender, then refresh quickly in iced water. Drain as soon as they are cold.

Cook the fava beans in boiling water for 1 minute, then refresh quickly in iced water and remove their skins.

Chop the onion finely and sauté in 3 tablespoons of the olive oil till lightly colored. Add the artichoke quarters, 1 cup water, the garlic, the fennel, carrots, fennel seeds, marjoram, salt and pepper. Simmer gently, removing each vegetable as it is cooked. Leave to cool. When they are all cooked, reduce the cooking liquid till you have ½ cup juice. Add a few drops of lemon juice and the basil. Leave to cool. Mix together all the ingredients (except the snow peas and cooking liquid) and add the rest of the olive oil.

Arrange the snow peas in a fan shape on each side of a serving plate. Place the rest of the vegetables in the center, as elegantly as possible. Decorate with a few sprigs of marjoram and pour the juice over.

Langoustines, endives and beet with marjoram

les langoustines aux endives et betteraves
à la marjolaine

The humor in this dish is made more apparent when the "bouquet" of marjoram flowers is placed between the claws. Marjoram is associated with weddings and the langoustines here take on the appearance of a bridesmaid.

ingredients

2 small zucchini

4 endives

4 tablespoons olive oil

salt and pepper

2 tablespoons white vermouth

7 tablespoons light cream

a pinch of curry powder

1 raw beet, peeled and cubed

1 shallot, diced

1 lemon

2 tablespoons chopped marjoram

4 tablespoons (½ stick) butter

12 raw langoustines (or prawns)

beet crisps to garnish (optional)

sprigs of flowering marjoram to garnish (optional)

method

Cut the zucchini into 3½-inch sections and slice finely lengthwise ⅛ inch thick) on a mandolin. Cook in boiling, salted water for 1 to 2 minutes, making sure they remain crisp. Refresh in iced water and drain at once. Cut the endives into quarters, then into ½-inch sections. Sauté in a frying pan with 2 tablespoons of the olive oil and salt and pepper, letting them caramelize, and stirring often. When they are golden, add the vermouth, cream and curry powder. Cook gently for a few minutes until the mixture thickens slightly.

Put the beet and shallot in a small pan with 1 tablespoon of the olive oil. Season with salt and pepper and add water just to cover. Cover and cook on a gentle heat for 15 minutes, stirring often. When the beet is cooked, liquefy in a blender with the cooking juices, the juice and zest of ½ of the lemon, the rest of the olive oil and the marjoram. Add 2 tablespoons of the butter and blend till smooth. Return the mixture to a pan and warm it through. Check the seasoning.

Remove the heads of the langoustines, reserving one for garnish. Peel and de-vein, season with salt and pepper and cook in a non-stick frying pan with the remaining butter for 2 or 3 minutes. Be careful not to overcook or they will lose much of their flavor. When cooked, squeeze some lemon juice over them. Arrange the zucchini slices in a fan shape on a serving plate and place the endives in the center, with the langoustines on top. Decorate with a langoustine head with crossed claws. Pour over the beet sauce. If you wish, you may decorate with some beet crisps (thin slices of beet fried in olive oil) and with some sprigs of marjoram.

Small red mullets with marjoram in red and black

les petits rougets à la marjolaine en rouge et noir

Red mullet is a good summer fish to eat as it has a light texture and is easily digestible.

ingredients

3 pinches saffron powder

3 pinches paprika

6 tablespoons olive oil

24 firm black Moroccan olives

6 large tomatoes, skinned and deseeded

1 red bell pepper

1 sweet onion, chopped

2 sprigs of marjoram

4 garlic cloves, peeled

salt and pepper

12 small red Mediterranean mullets (or mullet or any firm, white-fleshed fish), about 2½ ounces each (or 8 of 3½ ounce)

red chili peppers to decorate (optional)

method

Warm the saffron and paprika in 3 tablespoons of the olive oil for 1 minute on a gentle heat. Remove from the heat and leave to infuse.

Cut 12 of the olives into dice. Put in a pan with water, just to cover. Bring to the boil, drain and repeat the operation twice more.

Chop the tomatoes and bell pepper into small dice. Heat the remaining olive oil in a saucepan and add the chopped onion and bell pepper. Cook gently, then add the tomatoes, olives, half the marjoram leaves and 2 of the cloves of garlic, chopped. Season with salt and pepper and leave to simmer for 5 minutes.

In a frying pan, heat the infused oil. Add the remaining 2 garlic cloves, cut in quarters, and the rest of the marjoram. Let the oil become impregnated with these flavors, then add the red mullets and cook gently for 2 to 3 minutes on each side, depending on their size.

Serve the mullets on top of the black and red fondue of tomatoes and olives. Drizzle with the perfumed oil and decorate the plate with the remaining marjoram leaves and olives. The red chili peppers add color.

Thin tuna tart with marjoram vinaigrette

la tarte fine de thon à la vinaigrette de marjolaine

Tuna fish, once only found in the markets of the Mediterranean, is now available worldwide. The flesh is dark and firm and particularly suitable for broiling.

ingredients

8 ounces puff pastry dough

8 ounces fennel bulbs

salt and pepper

7 ounces thin green beans

14 ounces fresh tuna

1 tablespoon very finely chopped chives

leaves from 2 sprigs of marjoram

for the vinaigrette

2 tablespoons shallots, finely chopped

2 tablespoons sherry vinegar

2 tablespoons hazelnut oil

6 tablespoons olive oil

1 tablespoon tamarind juice or soy sauce

2 tablespoons diced beet

method

Roll out the dough very thinly on a cold marble slab and cut into 4 circles each 7 inches in diameter. Place the circles on a baking sheet and leave to rest in the refrigerator for an hour. Preheat the oven to 350°F. Bake the pastry bases in the preheated oven for 5 to 10 minutes or until golden. Supervise closely during cooking as pastry can burn very quickly.

Combine all the vinaigrette ingredients in a bowl and whisk. Finely slice the fennel and cook in boiling, salted water for 15 to 20 minutes. Refresh in cold water, drain, dry on a tea-towel, then season with salt and pepper. Cook the green beans in boiling, salted water for 5 to 6 minutes, depending on their thickness, then plunge into iced water, drain and season with a little of the vinaigrette, salt and pepper. Cut the tuna into escalopes $\frac{1}{8}$ inch thick, then place between 2 sheets of plastic wrap and flatten to $\frac{1}{16}$ inch thick.

To assemble the tart, place the fennel slices on the pastry, well spread out in a regular pattern. Carefully place the tuna on the fennel, without overlapping, but taking care to cover all the pastry. Season with salt and pepper.

Heat the grill. Place the baking tray on which the tarts are placed over a high heat for 30 seconds or so (in order to warm the base of the tarts) then cook under the grill. The tuna should be very rare.

Place the beans on a serving plate in the form of a notched wheel. Remove the tarts from the grill and place in the center. Warm the vinaigrette in a small pan and pour over the tart. Decorate with scattered chives and a few leaves of marjoram.

Rabbit roasted with marjoram and sauté of girolles mushrooms with potatoes and white beans

le petit lapin rôti à la marjolaine en cocotte
avec son sauté de girolles au pomme de terre et haricots blancs

If you are lucky enough to find it, an aromatic, smooth Vallée des Baux olive oil is my choice to complement the flavor of the girolles.

ingredients

1 young rabbit, 2½ pounds

3 small white potatoes

salt and pepper

6 tablespoons Provençal olive oil

1 pound girolle mushrooms, cleaned

4 tablespoons (½ stick) butter

6 garlic cloves, chopped

1 ounce smoked slab bacon, rind removed and
  cut into strips 1 inch wide and ¼ inch thick

1 small onion, finely chopped

1 tablespoon white wine

⅔ cup dried white cannellini beans,
  soaked overnight and drained

1 sprig of thyme

1 sprig of marjoram

1 bay leaf

5 sprigs of flat-leaf parsley

method

Cut the rabbit into pieces: the saddle in 4, the thighs and front legs in 2, liver and kidneys. Cook the potatoes in their skins in salted water until tender. Leave to cool, then cut them in half, sprinkle with salt, pepper and olive oil, and broil them on a cast-iron grill. Sauté the girolles in 3 tablespoons of the butter and a little olive oil in a non-stick frying pan, adding salt and pepper and 1 of the chopped garlic cloves.

In a casserole, heat 2 tablespoons of the olive oil and sauté the rabbit pieces and the bacon on a high heat until brown. Season with salt and pepper, then add the onion, simmer for 5 minutes, then add the wine and the remaining garlic. Reduce for 2 to 3 minutes, add 2¼ cups of water, remove the rabbit and reserve. Add the beans to the saucepan, bring to the boil and boil rapidly for 10 minutes, then cook for a further 35 minutes or until tender. Return the rabbit to the pan with the thyme, marjoram and bay leaf. Simmer for 5 minutes, then add the girolles.

Put a little of the cooking liquid into a blender with 1 tablespoon of the olive oil, the rest of the butter, the parsley leaves, salt and pepper. Blend until you have a very smooth pale green sauce. Place the sauce in a small pan and warm to tepid. Arrange the rabbit and vegetables on a serving plate. Decorate with a few marjoram leaves and a trickle of the green sauce.

Almond and marjoram mirliton with citrus fruits

le mirliton d'amande et de marjolaine aux agrumes

It is important to boil the orange rind strips as this removes all trace of bitterness.

ingredients

1 orange

3 pink grapefruit

2 tablespoons granulated sugar

2 sprigs of marjoram, plus extra to decorate

1 vanilla bean

a pinch of cornstarch

for the mirliton

scant ½ cup finely ground blanched
 almonds

1¼ cups fromage blanc

5 tablespoons sugar

a few drops of lemon juice

4 mint leaves

2 tablespoons olive oil

1 tablespoon Amaretto liqueur

blanched almonds, to decorate

method

Cut the rind very thinly from the orange and cut into matchstick strips. Put them in a small pan, cover with cold water, bring to the boil, then drain. Repeat twice.

Peel the orange and grapefruit, removing all the pith. Remove the segments with a very sharp knife, discarding the skin and pips. Do this over a saucepan to catch the juices. Liquefy the orange segments, the juices, sugar and marjoram leaves until very smooth. Return to the saucepan and add the strips of orange rind and the vanilla bean, halved and with its seeds scraped out. Cook for 5 to 6 minutes, then thicken very slightly with the cornstarch and cool rapidly. Remove the vanilla bean. Cut it in 4 for decoration if you like. Strain the juice, reserving the orange rind.

To make the mirliton, liquefy all the ingredients except the blanched almonds for 1 to 2 minutes till very smooth. Place in a suitable container and freeze. When ready to serve, scrape and crush the mixture with a fork to obtain small crystals. Press the crystals into a round bottomless mold 3 inches in diameter in the center of a serving plate. Pour the citrus juice around it, add the grapefruit segments and sprinkle the orange rind strips over the top. Decorate with blanched almonds and sprigs of marjoram.

the herb
winter savory
at the palme d'or

Winter savory, *Satureia montana*, or *sarriette* as it is known in France, is looked upon as a "happy" herb, and the reason for this is its reputation as an aphrodisiac. Its generic name stems from the Latin *satyrus*, suggesting its importance as an offering to Bacchus, the god of wine and licentious behavior, during Roman orgies. For this very reason monks in early France were forbidden to grow the "herb of love" in their gardens.

Introduced into Provence by the Romans, it is an indigenous hardy perennial found growing wild on sunny hillsides and along pathways all along the Mediterranean coasts from Italy to southern Spain. It grows low to the ground in the wild and, as a result, you are often not aware of it until you tread on it, crushing the leaves and releasing the delightful scent. As an edging plant it releases its fragrance as you brush past it and its flowers are much loved by bees. It has soft white flowers very similar to thyme, throughout the summer, being of the same Labiatae family. But there the similarity ends. Unlike thyme it does not retain all its leaves in the cold winter months but produces new leaf each year. M. Leuranguer, the chef at the Palme d'Or, only discovered this herb when he moved from Brittany. When I first met him he assured me that it was so versatile a herb that he could produce countless recipes for desserts alone.

cultivation

Winter savory grows to a height of 4 to16 inches and prefers a light, poor, but well-drained soil in full sun. It is a compact, hardy perennial sub-shrub which benefits from a good clipping before winter and a relatively hard prune, back to 4 inches in the early spring, when it will produce new leaf and bush out again. Avoid the temptation to mulch, as it hates damp conditions. It is a tough little plant and responds well if planted in a rough terrain. Seed should be sown in late summer or spring and mature plants can be divided in mid-spring. Softwood cuttings can be taken in the summer months. There are two other savories that can be cultivated: *Satureia hortensis*, or summer savory, and a creeping variety called *Satureia spicigera*. Harvest the leaves and flowers of winter savory at any time during the growing season.

culinary uses

In Germany winter savory is known as "*Bohnenkraut,*" or "bean-herb," since it makes all beans more easily digestible. It has a calming effect on the stomach, giving rise to its country name in France, "*poor folk's sauce.*" Savory is a stimulating herb and therefore excites the appetite, especially in fruit desserts and anything with ice cream. It has a strong flavor and should be used judiciously, like so many of our *herbes de Provence*. Depending upon your taste, you can add it chopped finely to scrambled eggs, devilled eggs, strong sauces, stuffings for poultry and all kinds of green bean or lentil soups. It adds an extra piquancy to roast meats if sprinkled over at the last moment.

the restaurant
palme d'or

For those of you who regret the passing of that age of elegance so evocatively captured in F. Scott Fitzgerald's *Tender is the Night*, a visit to the Thirties-style Hôtel Martinez, Cannes, is essential. If you also wish to experience the epitome of elegance in cuisine at this most luxurious location on the Bay of Cannes, then you have to dine at the Palme d'Or restaurant. This elevated room, named in honor of the famous top award at the Cannes Film Festival, has an outstanding view, beyond towering palm trees, of the azure blue sea, and places you in the company of the stars that made the Hollywood film business a dream factory. Here, on the walls, given pride of place, are unique black and white publicity photographs of, among others, Marilyn Monroe, Greta Garbo, Marlene Dietrich, Cary Grant, Clark Gable, Humphrey Bogart and Leslie Caron.

Settling down into one of the comfortable armchairs at a table overlooking the Art Deco style swimming pool, it is hard to believe that only twenty years ago this room was nothing more than a storage attic. It was suggested the room be put to better use. The chef de cuisine, still at the Martinez, M. Christian Willer, came up with the idea of the Palme d'Or.

The secret of the success of the Palme d'Or restaurant kitchen is in its team spirit. This may seem an obvious statement, since all our restaurants rely on the brigade working well together, but in this extremely busy kitchen everyone gets a chance to show their true potential. Our herbs were hand-delivered by a rotund, jocular farmer who grows his plants in the hills above Nice. He was welcomed in the kitchens as if he were the most important guest in the hotel. The herbs were examined and approved by as many as three chefs. The selection included fennel, thyme, rosemary and marjoram as well as the savory we need for our special recipes. M. Leuranguer handled the brittle stems with reverence in order not to damage the soft white flowers or bruise the leaves before using them. All around us the young chefs were busy preparing for luncheon. There was a tiny desk littered with the morning's receipts and scribbled instructions. On the main noticeboard there was a menu to be prepared, in two weeks time, for one of the most respected vineyards in the south of France, the Domaine Ott. Nothing here can be left to chance. There is a reputation to consider. Although welcome, I was suddenly aware that the pace was quickening around me and I was careful to keep clear of the narrow corridors between work surfaces.

I eased around a corner to where the pastries were being prepared. It was then that I noticed the steep staircase up which all meals to the Palme d'Or were carried. The waiters will, no doubt, be grateful for the new kitchens, being constructed beyond the wall behind me, which will make for more space and easier access. I must add a mention of the plates at the Palme d'Or. Each of our restaurants has its own distinctive tableware in keeping with the house style and the Palme d'Or is no exception. All around the perimeter of the plates are inscribed the names of the winners of the coveted prize at the Cannes Film Festival and the dates of their award. It makes fascinating reading.

the chef
jean-yves leuranguer

The letters M.O.F. (which M. Leuranguer has after his name) literally translated mean "Top workman of France." It sounds rather incongruous, which is why literal translations are sometimes unhelpful. In fact "Maître Ouvrier de France" is one of the highest honors bestowed on a young chef. M. Leuranguer is quietly spoken and listens intently. In his presence you feel assured by his calm approach and a little in awe of him. He is polite and quietly formal in manner, but as you get to know him you become aware of his gentle sense of humor. After dinner he told me that he lived with his wife and family at a nearby village called Biot, close to Antibes. "This former village has so much been encroached upon by the expanding environs of Antibes that the residents of Biot are now being renamed 'Antibiotics'." His wit is intelligent, as is his approach to the art of cooking, and with him cooking is very much an art.

After working, in his youth, in three restaurants in Paris, he returned to be near his parents at Brest in Brittany. But he dreamed of a career in the south of France. Thanks to a friend who was working at the Palais des Festivals, the home to the Cannes Film Festival, he heard of a post going vacant working alongside a rising star of the Côte d'Azur, Christian Willer, at the Hôtel Martinez. That was fourteen years ago.

They make the perfect team. M. Willer is outgoing and creative in an expansive way and M. Leuranguer is introspective and creative in a quietly authoritative manner. Even in the absence of M. Willer there is no doubt as to who is in charge. He encourages *esprit de corps* and delights in his colleagues' talents. We were able to enjoy the inventiveness of the dessert chef, M. Frédéric Poisson, without a hint of rivalry between them. The end result was looked upon as a joint triumph, and a glass of Taittinger champagne at the end of the working day was raised to the team's efforts. M. Leuranguer then confided in me that he was about to take a vacation with his family. It was to be the first time in three years that they would all gather around the same table for dinner.

Dedication and hard work inevitably lead to sacrifices for the family. Being a top chef is not a job for the faint-hearted.

"Team spirit is of the essence."

Fava bean and savory soup

soupe de fèves à la sarriette

This is a classic soup from Provence, tailor-made for winter savory.

serves
ten

ingredients

2 cups shelled petits peas
  (1¼ to 1½ pounds in pods)
2 cups shelled fava beans
  (2 to 2¼ pounds in pods)
1 sprig of savory
1 quart strong chicken stock
1 teaspoon sugar
1 tablespoon cornstarch
3 cups whipping cream
10 to 12 tablespoons (2½ to 3 sticks) butter
salt and pepper

for the garnish
10 young onions, about 1½ ounces each
2 to 4 tablespoons ricotta cheese
2 to 4 tablespoons mascarpone cheese
1½ tablespoons shelled fava beans, lightly
  cooked
1 tablespoon butter
olive oil
sea salt
savory leaves
5 fennel tops or one small bulb, cooked
2 thin slices of prosciutto

method

Cook the peas in salted, boiling water till they are soft. Refresh in cold water. Drain. Do the same with the fava beans, adding the sprig of savory.

Purée both peas and fava beans in a blender. Bring the stock to the boil with the sugar in a large saucepan, pour in the purée and whisk together. Reduce the heat and simmer for 1 minute. Mix a tablespoon of cornstarch with a little water and whisk into the simmering soup.

Add the cream, simmer for a further 2 minutes, then skim. Pour through a fine strainer into a large bowl. Add the butter and stir well. Check the seasoning and adjust if necessary.

To prepare the garnish, cook the onions in boiling water until tender. Mix the ricotta and mascarpone cheese together and form into quenelle shapes. Warm the fava beans in the butter. Use to garnish the soup, and add salt, olive oil and 4 to 5 leaves of savory. Make lozenges of the cooked fennel and prosciutto and serve separately.

Fried turbot with savory and caramelized tomatoes

turbot cuit au plat à la sarriette et tomates caramelisées

The flat-leafed parsley is a great favorite with cooks, because of its strong flavor. Often called "French" or "Italian" parsley, it can be grown anywhere if the soil is rich and well-drained.

serves
eight

ingredients

1 turbot, 8 to 9 pounds

6 firm ripe tomatoes, 6 to 7 ounces each

salt

1 tablespoon granulated sugar

1 tablespoon all-purpose flour

1 tablespoon olive oil

2 tablespoons butter

8 sprigs of winter savory

basil leaves to decorate

for the parsley coulis

1½ cups button mushrooms

7 tablespoons chicken stock

1 bunch of flat-leafed parsley

salt and pepper

for the savory sauce

¾ cup chopped shallots

1 cup white wine

4 tablespoons white-wine vinegar

2 cups (4 sticks) butter

leaves from 1 small sprig of savory

salt and pepper

lemon juice

2 tablespoons capers, chopped

⅔ cup black Nice olives, sliced lengthwise

1 bunch each of tarragon, chives and chervil, chopped

to cook the fish

4 tablespoons olive oil

4 tablespoons (½ stick) butter

method

Divide the turbot into 8 portions, removing the skin. Skin, cut in half, and seed the tomatoes. Sprinkle with salt and sugar and dust lightly with strained flour. Cook in a frying pan with olive oil and butter until caramelized.

To make the parsley coulis, simmer the mushrooms in the chicken stock. Liquefy the flat-leafed parsley. Liquefy the mushrooms with their cooking juices and add the parsley juice. Season.

To make the savory sauce, simmer the shallots with the white wine and vinegar in the butter until soft, then put through a fine strainer. Dice 4 of the caramelized half tomatoes and add, together with the savory leaves, salt, pepper and lemon juice. Reserve. Just before serving, add the capers, olives, tarragon, chives and chervil.

Fry the turbot in a pan in olive oil and butter. To serve, place a caramelized half tomato at the top of each plate and garnish with a basil leaf. Place the fish in the center, speared with a sprig of savory and surrounded by the sauce.

Ravioli and artichoke hearts with savory

ravioli et effeuillé d'artichauts à la sarriette

ingredients

5 large globe artichokes

3 ounces goat's cheese

1½ ounces Jambon de Bayonne or prosciutto, diced

a small branch of savory, with flowers if possible

salt and pepper

7 tablespoons olive oil

3½ ounces fresh pasta dough

2¼ cups white wine

⅓ cup finely chopped onions

⅔ cup finely chopped carrots

2 cloves of garlic, finely chopped

5 small violet or provençal artichokes

1 bunch of arugula

1 endive heart

a small bunch of cilantro

2 tablespoons balsamic vinegar

½ cup skinned, seeded and diced tomatoes

method

Remove the outer leaves and choke from the large artichokes and cut into quarters. Simmer in boiling water until tender, then purée them in a blender. Mix together the goat's cheese, diced ham, half the artichoke purée, 2 finely chopped leaves of savory, salt, pepper and half the olive oil. Roll out the pasta dough thinly and cut out 40 circles each 1¼ inches in diameter. Divide the filling between 20 of the circles, put the remaining circles on top and pinch the edges to seal.

Put the remaining oil in a large pan with the wine, onions, carrots and garlic to make a barigoule sauce. Bring to the boil, add 4 of the violet artichokes and simmer until tender. Remove from the pan reserving the liquid and cut the artichokes into quarters. Slice the last violet artichoke and pan-fry in a little oil. Poach the ravioli in the barigoule liquid. Place the remaining artichoke purée in the center of the serving dish, decorated with quarters of artichokes barigoule. Surround with the ravioli.

Sauté the salad leaves briefly and sprinkle over the dish with the cilantro. Add the balsamic vinegar and diced tomatoes to the barigoule liquid and pour over the dish. Scatter the fried artichoke slices over the top, and sprinkle with savory flowers if you have them. Top with a sprig of savory.

Saddle of milk-fed lamb in a salt crust with herb salad

canon d'agneau de lait marine en croûte de sel
salade d'herbes

A saddle of lamb will weigh about 6 pounds. You might wish to halve this for 4 people, or ask your butcher's advice.

ingredients

1 cup (2 sticks) butter

chopped garlic

savory leaves

1 saddle of milk-fed lamb

salt and pepper

1 pound chard, or spinach leaves

4 large tomatoes, peeled and seeded

for the salt crust

4 ounces sea salt

1⅔ cups all-purpose flour

a bunch of herbs, including bay leaves,
     thyme, savory, rosemary

2 egg whites

4 tablespoons all-purpose flour

method

To make the salt crust, mix together the ingredients and leave for 2 hours.

Mix the butter and garlic with a little savory. Spread half the butter over the lamb and leave to marinate for 2 hours. Season the lamb lightly and brown in a frying pan over a high heat. Leave to cool on a rack.

Preheat the oven to 400°F. Coat the lamb with the rest of the creamed butter. Blanch the chard or spinach leaves and wrap around the lamb. Roll out the salt crust with a rolling pin, place the lamb at one end and roll up. Roast in the preheated oven for 10 minutes for pink or 15 minutes for medium cooked. Serve with the tomatoes, sprinkled with savory, accompanied by a herb salad (see below).

salade d'herbes

ingredients

sprigs and leaves of

chervil, basil, tarragon, dill, mint, marjoram, chives, cilantro, purslane, curly endive

2 tablespoons balsamic vinegar

salt and pepper

method

Put all the sprigs and leaves into a bowl and dress with the balsamic vinegar, salt and pepper.

Pigeons perfumed with savory flowers under the skin, split and broiled with sweet garlic and wild mushrooms

pigeonneau parfumé à la fleur de sarriette sous la peau
grillé en crapaudine à l'ail doux, avec champignons sauvages

The winter savory should be chopped very finely. The freshly harvested green garlic has a less pungent flavor, so as not to overpower the perfume of the savory flowers.

ingredients

14 tablespoons (1¾ sticks) butter
1 bunch of flowering savory
4 pigeons, 1 pound each
2 bulbs of new season garlic
7 ounces olive oil
7 ounces girolles (or chanterelles) mushrooms
4 sprigs of savory to garnish
young carrots and fava beans to serve

method

Make a savory butter by creaming most of the butter and stir in the chopped savory leaves, keeping back a few flowers for decoration.

Split the pigeons vertically from tip of breast to wings. Spread the savory butter over the breasts and under the skin.

Peel the garlic cloves. Blanch 3 times in boiling water, then drain, put the garlic in a bowl and cover with olive oil. Set aside. Clean the mushrooms and fry in the remaining butter.

Brown the garlic cloves in a frying pan with a little olive oil. Broil the pigeons, skin side to heat source, then place in a medium oven till cooked through. Serve each pigeon with the garlic and mushrooms around it. Decorate with a sprig of savory. Serve with young carrots and fava beans, and hand the juices in a sauceboat.

Apple confit with savory, vanilla ice cream and crispy pastries

pomme confite
à la sarriette
crème glacée à la vanille, arlettes croustillantes

French Golden Delicious is particularly good in this recipe, but any crisp, white-fleshed apple can be substituted.

serves ten

ingredients

5 large Golden Delicious apples
1 cup granulated sugar
6 tablespoons (¾ stick) butter
3 sprigs savory
1 cup whipping cream

for the crispy pastries
10 ounces puff pastry dough
a little melted butter
confectioners' sugar

for the vanilla ice cream
1 quart milk
7 ounces whipping cream
12 egg yolks
1¾ cups plus 2 tablespoons granulated
  sugar
3 vanilla beans

method

To make the vanilla ice cream, make a custard with the milk, cream, egg yolks, sugar and the vanilla beans. Leave to cool, remove the vanilla, then churn in an ice-cream making machine.

Peel and core the apples, cut each one in 8, cook in a pan with ½ cup of granulated sugar until the sugar has melted, then add the butter and a sprig of savory. Cook gently for 10 to 15 minutes.

To make the crispy pastries, preheat the oven to 350°F. Roll out the pastry very thinly. Brush with a little melted butter and roll it up. Leave to rest, then cut into 20 to 30 slices ¼ inch thick. Roll out very thinly and sprinkle with confectioners' sugar. Bake in the preheated oven for 10 minutes till well caramelized.

Make a caramel with ½ cup granulated sugar. When well colored, add the cream and 2 sprigs of savory. Leave to infuse.

On each plate, place 4 pieces of apple, a quenelle of vanilla ice cream, 2 or 3 pastries and some caramel savory sauce.

Gelatin mold of red fruits, sabayon with savory

gelée de fruits rouges, sabayon à la sarriette

Wild strawberries, *fraises de bois*, can be grown in temperate climates, often going under the name alpine strawberries.

serves
ten

ingredients

1¾ cups water

2 cups ripe strawberries

3 leaves of gelatin

1 ounce pectin

7 ounces raspberries

1 pint red fruit sorbet

7 ounces wild strawberries

orange slices to decorate

savory sprigs to decorate

for the sabayon

10 egg yolks

10 tablespoons water

6 tablespoons granulated sugar

3 or 4 savory leaves

method

Bring the water to the boil, then add 1½ pounds of the ripe strawberries and leave to infuse for 1 hour off the heat. Meanwhile soak the gelatin leaves in water to soften.

Pass the strawberries through a strainer to remove the seeds. Heat the resulting syrup in a saucepan and add the pectin. Bring to the boil, then remove from the heat and add the softened gelatin. Leave to rest until cold, but not set.

Place the remaining strawberries with the raspberries in serving glasses. Pour over the gelatin mixture and leave to set in the refrigerator.

To make the sabayon, whisk together the egg yolks, water and sugar very carefully in a bowl over hot water, adding very finely chopped savory at the end.

Add a ball of red fruit sorbet to each glass, with a few wild strawberries and some sabayon. Decorate with orange slices and skewers of wild strawberries and finish with a soft sprig of savory.

restaurant details

Auberge de Noves ★
Route de Châteaurenard
13550 Noves
Bouches-de-Rhône
Telephone: 04 90 24 28 28
Fax: 04 90 90 16 92
e-mail: noves@relaischateaux.fr

Oustau de Baumanière ★★
13520 Les Baux de Provence
Bouches-de-Rhône
Telephone: 04 90 54 33 07
Fax: 04 90 54 40 46
e-mail: oustau@relaischateaux.fr

Auberge la Fenière ★
Route de Cadenet—BP 18
84160 Lourmarin
Vaucluse
Telephone: 04 90 68 11 79
Fax: 04 90 68 18 60
e-mail: Reine@wanadoo.fr

La Bastide de Moustiers
Chemin de Quinson
64360 Moustiers-Sainte-Marie
Alpes-de-Haute-Provence
Telephone: 04 92 70 47 47
Fax: 04 92 70 47 48
e-mail: labastide@alain-ducasse.com

Chez Bruno ★
Route de Vidauban
83510 Lorgues
Var
Telephone: 04 94 85 93 93
Fax: 04 94 85 93 99

La Bastide Saint-Antoine ★★
48, avenue Henri Dunant
06130 Grasse
Telephone: 04 93 70 94 94
Fax: 04 93 70 94 95
e-mail: info@jacques-chibois.com

Palme d'Or ★★
Hotel Martinez
73, La Croisette
06406 Cannes
Telephone: 04 92 98 73 00
Fax: 04 93 39 03 38
e-mail: martinez@concorde-hotels.com

★ Michelin stars correct at the time of going to press